Assateague Island

D1559156

A Guide to
Assateague Island National Seashore
Maryland and Virginia

Produced by the
Division of Publications
National Park Service

U.S. Department of the Interior
Washington, D.C.

Using This Handbook
Assateague Island National Seashore lies off the
coasts of Maryland and Virginia. Major attractions
are seashore recreation, bird life, the wild ponies,
diminutive Sika deer, surf fishing, and the nature of
an Atlantic Coast barrier island itself. Part 1 of this
handbook introduces the area's history. Part 2 ex-
plores the natural history of the barrier island and of
Chincoteague National Wildlife Refuge, and inter-
prets the behavior of the ponies.

National Park Handbooks are compact introduc-
tions to the great natural and historic places adminis-
tered by the National Park Service. They are published to support the National Park Service's management programs and to help you understand and
enjoy the parks. Each is intended to be informative
reading and a useful guide before, during, and after a
park visit. This is Handbook 106.

Library of Congress Cataloging in Publication Data
United States. National Park Service.
Assateague Island National Seashore, Maryland and
Virginia.
(National park handbook; 106)
"A barrier island natural history, by William H.
Amos" p.
Bibliography: p.
Supt. of Docs. no.: I 29.9/5:106
1. Assateague Island National Seashore, Md, and
Va. I. Amos, William Hopkins. II. Title. III. Series:
United States. National Park Service.
Handbook—National Park Service; 106.
F187.A84U53   1980   917.52′21   79-607136

For sale by the Superintendent of Documents, U.S.
Government Printing Office, Washington, DC 20402
☆ GPO: 1985—311- 340/2   Reprint 1999

Contents

Welcome to Assateague

Preceding pictures: Assateague Island embraces the sun and fun of family beach recreation; shorebird acrobatics; bursts of wild pony energy in the surf; and the Atlantic's many moods, including fogbound intimacy. Our cover: A common tern prepares to make a food offering in courtship ritual.

Wind and Weather, Ponies and Pirates

We love to sit on the beach, or better yet squat on our haunches at water's edge and stare out at the vast ocean, feeling torn between the land and water. What fascinates us as we perform this ritual up and down the beach is one of nature's three great confrontations, the endless give and take between earth's solidity and water's constancy of movement. Nature's other confrontations, between land and air, and water and air, are more subtle. They are at work here at Assateague, of course, but we cannot stand with one foot in each as we can where ocean and sandy beach come together.

The shore announces a great transition, thereby declaring itself an obvious setting for recreation and vacation. Nature here urges us to shift our modes and reflect on our origins and continuity with the mineral, plant, and animal kingdoms. Gulls, terns, and willets wing above, crabs crawl below. The things of life take place right before our eyes, strong, often beautiful, and elemental.

As a barrier island fronting the ocean this remains today the first land in America, as it was for Colonel Henry Norwood on January 3, 1650. He and a party of seafarers put ashore just north of here from a storm-wracked ship, hoping to find fresh water, food, and a likely harbor for making repairs to the ship, which was bound for the Virginia colony from England via the West Indies. They found water and oysters and fowl for food, but the next morning the ship set sail without them, for reasons about which Norwood's account, later published in England, only speculates. They were eventually rescued and transported to the mainland by friendly Indians. They completed the journey to the young Virginia colony on foot, but not before deaths, cannibalism, and near total despair had set in. "And thus we wish'd every day to be the last of our lives (if God had so pleased), so hopeless and desperate was our condition, all expectation of human succour being vanished and gone," Norwood laments in his *A Voyage to Virginia.*

Norwood's account gives one of the best descriptions we have of this area's Indians, who graciously received the destitute and forlorn newcomers and presumably also assured them safe passage to Virginia and Jamestown. Except for occasional arrowheads in the surf, today's only reminders of the Indian presence here are the many names adopted from their expressive languages by Europeans: Assateague and Chincoteague, Nanticoke and Pocomoke, and Wicomico. History, folklore, and archeology are unfortunately silent regarding these Indians, and no one thought to study their culture systematically until long after the Indians were thoroughly dispossessed of their lands. By the early 1700s the Assateagues had already been pressured north into what is now Delaware. Endless dealings and posturings between the Maryland colony and various Indian groups are preserved in *The Archives of Maryland*, but these shed only indirect light on the lives, thoughts, and practices of these tribes of common Algonkian language stock. Assateague's Indians were largely seasonal visitors who came to the area to gather the harvest of the sea, estuaries, and marshes. They did not attempt to pit their lives against the forces of the environment here during the most trying parts of the year. Many subsequent attempts at farming and stock raising here by settlers would eventually founder because of periodic severe conditions.

Norwood is also our first storm chronicler for the Assateague area. The storm he recounts would not have been a hurricane because it developed outside the tropics, and hurricanes, first reported in the New World by Columbus in 1493, originate in the tropics. But storms like Norwood's, although less numerous than hurricanes, can be equally as destructive. In fact, the worst storm of this century here, occurring in March, 1962, was an extratropical cyclone that occurred at maximum range spring tides. Hurricanes do batter the shores repeatedly here. They struck most harrowingly in 1933, 1954 (Hazel), and twice in 1955 (Connie and Diane). The Inlet Storm or Great '33 Hurricane cut the peninsula through at Ocean City, Maryland, and a jetty was built to keep the inlet open. Connie and Diane dumped one-third of the region's *annual* average precipitation between August 12 and August 18. A 1936 hurricane let fall nearly a quarter of the annual average precipitation in just 28 hours. But loss of human life to storms has been fortunately low in this region, compared with

The original Assateague Lighthouse used a candle lantern. Today's tower was built in 1867 and equipped with an oilburning lamp that was replaced with a revolving electric light in 1963. The lighthouse sits far inland now because of natural changes in the island. Its light can be seen for 19 nautical miles.

many coastal areas.

Ships and storms will sometimes equal wrecks and Assateague has seen its share. In recent years large crafts have been blown aground and broken up by the surf off the south end of the island. Most of the wrecks of sailing ships and barges are strewn about the island, buried by shifting sand. Occasional storms remove sufficient sand to newly expose a wreck to view.

Wrecks became almost a way of life on Assateague for a time. Salvaging cargo from wrecked or disabled ships in the early days was pursued at first to prevent the total waste of items ranging from molasses and bananas to silver, sugar, rum, bricks, and preserved meats. Those who found and buried dead sailors were paid one pound per corpse by the authorities. Salvaging wrecks got to be a paraprofessional pasttime for some, however, and Maryland and Virginia eventually moved to halt the practice. One particularly provoking incident involved the Spanish ship *Greyhound* in the 18th century. Overly ardent salvagers stripped it not only of its cargo, including a shipment of mahogany, but also of its very timbers. In 1782 a Commissioner of Wrecks office was created in Virginia and some years later Maryland appointed a wreckmaster. With the coming of the Life Saving Service to these shores, the predecessor of the United States Coast Guard, the wreckmaster function became obsolete.

Wrecks and storms have provided the traditional explanation for the origins of the famous Chincoteague ponies of Assateague Island. Popular legend has held that they are the offspring of stock from the ill-fated ship *Greyhound,* but no hard evidence supports this idea.

No one is certain when the first horses were brought to Assateague. Historians do know that as early as the 17th century barrier islands were being used by colonists for grazing horses and cattle. Apparently this was done when damage to mainland crops by free-roaming animals became so great that colonial legislators levied taxes on all livestock and required that the animals be fenced.

Horses have been brought to and removed from Assateague many times. The resulting mix of bloodlines has produced the wide variety of colors and patterns in today's herds. The horses on Assateague's Virginia portion are often called Chincoteague ponies because many of their ancestors lived there or were

Life-saving station crewmen were called surfmen. They risked their lives in deadly surf to save the shipwrecked. Four stations were operated within the national seashore. The Life Saving Service was predecessor to the United States Coast Guard.

owned by that island's residents. Every year the Virginia herd returns to Chincoteague Island for a festive event known as Pony Penning.

In the 17th century, unmarked and unpenned horses could be claimed if captured and marked in the presence of neighbors. That practice probably initiated Pony Penning, which continues on the last Wednesday and Thursday of each July. The Virginia herd, owned by the Chincoteague Volunteer Fire Company since the 1920's, swims the channel then to Chincoteague, where many of the year's foals are sold at auction. Bids depend on an animal's appearance and on how many can be sold that year. The average bid is around $525. New owners buy a bit of Assateague history and usually find that the foals readily adapt to new environments and are easily domesticated.

Pirates and their treasures also have cloaked Assateague's history in mystery and intrigue. No less a pirate than Edward Teach, alias Blackbeard, haunted these parts, reputedly having one of his 14 wives domiciled on Assateague. He used Chincoteague Inlet and other inside waterways to gain access to the protected bay areas.

Charles Wilson, a former South Carolina sea captain who turned pirate, was condemned by the Admiralty Court and hanged in London in the mid-18th century. He had also used Assateague as a base of operations and left behind an enticing letter to his brother that surfaced in Germany in the 1940s. It leaves instructions for finding substantial treasures of gold, jewels and diamonds, and bars of silver on a bluff overlooking the Atlantic at the head of a creek north of an inlet above Chincoteague Island. The letter instructs the brother to go in secret and remove the ten chests. The brother died in this country, penniless. Efforts to find the treasure have been fruitless. Much of Assateague's piracy lore, of course, is pure legend, but the romance and mystery of daring pirates and buried treasures still excite the imagination.

Treasures of sea and bay brought people to live on the island eventually. Not the least of these were wildfowl. Early Maryland colonists, who settled due west of here in the middle portion of the Chesapeake Bay, registered sheer amazement at the birdlife they found. An account from the mid-1600s speaks of waterfowl "in millionous multitudes." Nor were the descriptions always appreciative. An early Marylander

said birds sat so thick on the water that they looked like "a mass of filth or turf."

A great egret and its reflection appear to idle in placid waters. Actually it stands alert to any food source passing within reach of its snaking neck and lightning, accurate bill.

Bird hunting and egg collecting of staggering proportions eventually threatened entire populations of these wild creatures whose plenitude had amazed the early settlers. The dire plight of the snow goose led to creation of the Chincoteague National Wildlife Refuge on the south end of Assateague Island in 1943. It occupies a strategic location along the Atlantic flyway, the migration route for numerous species, including Canada geese, peregrine falcons, and monarch butterflies. Many wild creatures have made or are making fine comebacks because they are now protected where they were once relentlessly slaughtered with swivel cannons and multiple punt guns. Hunters sometimes blasted away at the birds until their shoulders went raw from the recoil of their weapons. Wildfowling weaponry and antique decoys are displayed at the Wildfowl Museum in Salisbury, Maryland, along with carvings by contemporary artists.

The abandoned oyster house you can see across Toms Cove testifies to the value placed on the local oyster population. Full-time oyster watches were maintained over the cove for at least 85 years. Settlement eventually came to Assateague Beach and Pope Island, North Beach and Green Run when city demands for oysters, clams, wildfowl, and the diamond-back terrapin made the collecting of them profitable. Later a fish factory for processing menhaden into oil and fertilizer was built by the Seaboard Oil and Guano Company. After it was destroyed by fire another factory was built by the Conant Brothers close to the site. This factory operated until about 1929 when dramatic changes in Toms Cove prevented large ships from entering the cove. At low tide you can go clamming around the battered brick ruins of the first factory structure on the island's bay side in Toms Cove. A storm destroyed the fish factory, and the constantly shifting sands ruined the regionally famous oyster beds in Toms Cove proper. In fact, the whole nature of the south end of Assateague Island has changed dramatically in the last hundred years with the addition of "The Hook." Today's somewhat inland location of the lighthouse hints at this. Piles of shells adorn the waterfront just off main street in today's Chincoteague, where oystering and clamming boats still dock. But the boats are now ocean-going, rather

Preceding pages: A family celebrates summer's seashore rites by camping at Assateague.

than bay foragers. The taste for these delicate morsels of bay and sea has not changed, just the methods of securing them.

Another harvest of the sea here for a time was salt, which was tremendously important before refrigeration. Massive quantities of salt were used to preserve food; it was once so scarce that its value approximated that of gold. During the American Revolution period virtually all domestic salt production was accomplished by solar evaporation from clay lined pits or by boiling the seawater in kettles and wrought iron pans. By 1776 planters and farmers used prodigious quantities of salt for livestock and for curing meats for expanding urban populations. Medicine and a burgeoning seafood industry also consumed their shares. The British naval blockade of Atlantic ports easily shut off European salt supplies to the colonies, and colonists along the Atlantic seaboard rushed to meet the demand. Seawater is only three percent salt, so much boiling was required. The best documented colonial saltwork on Assateague Island was at Sinepuxent Inlet, an inlet long since naturally closed. These forms of salt making, dependent on good weather, died with the discovery of large underground salt deposits eleswhere that could be readily and cheaply mined.

Salt-making is gone, but concern about *weather* remains. An often-asked question is "What is the weather going to be like the weekend I plan to be at Assateague?" It can be answered no better here than by your local extended weather forecast or an explanation of a map of prevailing fronts. As the cliche suggests, the reports are as changeable as . . . well, the weather. And even "bad" seashore weather can provide a fruitful experience of Assateague Island if you take it in stride and use common sense about safety. The rainy beach presents a different world than the sunny beach, a world of increased subtlety for the senses. It is a smaller, closer world conveying an exhilarating sense of power and purpose that transcends the human. A sense of the vastness of the planet replaces feelings of locality. Waiting out a driving rainstorm can be—depending on your frame of mind—an unexpected blessing of free, unstructured time.

But rest assured that there is much good weather, too. The winds that sometimes bring rain and blow down tents in "foul" weather are also the winds that carry kites aloft to dot the airy canvas at water's edge with brightly colored forms and faces sporting streamers in the breeze. And the bright seashore sun puts the final, drying touches on the latest project of sandcastle architects of all ages—as well as burning careless or dozing sunbathers.

Swimming, sunbathing, surfing, shell collecting, fishing, and beachwalking on the ocean side; clamming, crabbing, camping, and canoeing on the bay side . . . Assateague Island unfolds a seashore world of many recreations. But at some point you may want to sit alone at the seashore's invitation and stare at the ocean. Adopt whatever theory you choose about why you feel compelled to do so, but do so. Some postulate a genetic memory theory, believing that our salt cells retain residual memories of our ancestral origins as forms of life evolving out of the oceans. Some theorize a primal attraction, like that which draws people to a campfire at night, to the ocean rolling and heaving in the changing light. Still others feel we are drawn to the sense of time's passing conveyed by the sight and sound of inexorable natural movement. But like those who walk the beach without a kite, surfboard or fishing rod, you may just enjoy yourself, unencumbered by theories about why you do. This too is emphatically Assateague Island.

Introducing William H. Amos   *A trip across the is-land, from the beach to the bayshore, is a richly re-warding experience at Assateague Island National Seashore. In this section, William H. Amos serves as your guide for such a trip, interpreting the con-ditions and communities of each life zone you en-counter along the way.*

Amos, raised in the Orient, was initiated into ma-rine life observation on the shores of the Philippine Islands and the Inland Sea of Japan. He has stud-ied both freshwater and marine organisms. His ex-tensive magazine articles and books have been illustrated with many of his own photographs. He has been associated with the New York Zoological Society, a Smithsonian expedition, and marine lab-oratories in the United States and abroad.

A Land Built by Sea and Wind

Ours is a world of constant change—yet there appear to be few fundamental differences in our surroundings from year-to-year. Since a human lifetime is too short to span periods of profound geological change, we must read planetary history through messages hidden in the earth or embedded in the form and function of living things.

Assateague, the great barrier island stretching along the coasts of Maryland and Virginia, clearly has experienced dramatic alterations during storms in past years. But these changes are minor compared to events that have occurred during its long existence. If we could condense ten thousand years into a few brief moments, we would discover the Assateague of the distant past lying far seaward of its present location. It too would be long and low; but in condensed time, as in a speeded-up motion picture, we would watch it stretch and shorten and extend again. Caught in the grip of ocean currents swirling upon the continental shelf, it would writhe and twist. Inlets would break through and heal over repeatedly. Its shorefront would wear away; but marshes on the inner bay shore would keep pace by building into the bay, so the island would march toward the continent. The true continental shoreline across the bay would retreat to the west, the bay itself seeming to invade the land, maintaining open water between the migrating island and the land.

The events that have occurred in this barrier-island system since the last glacial age are due largely to fluctuations of sea level as great continental ice sheets melted and water returned to the ocean basins. Not only has the sea level risen, but the coast itself has become depressed from the weight of sediment deposited upon it. Enormous quantities of ice-scoured rocks and sand were carried down by huge prehistoric coastal rivers and estuaries, altering the contours of the now-submerged continental shelf. Over the years, sediment-laden currents escaping from the land cut deeply into the submerged continental slope to carve out great submarine canyons which today plunge steeply toward the depths of the abyssal plain far below.

Prevailing offshore ocean currents have removed sand and sediment from the beaches, only to re-deposit them in entirely new configurations elsewhere along the shore and beneath the surface. Because Assateague, like all other barrier islands, has been in slow retreat for thousands of years, we may assume that it will continue to retreat as the sea level keeps rising. None of man's attempts—miniscule in the geological scale of things—are going to alter the long-range pattern. The Assateague of today is only a temporary manifestation of events that have gone unchecked for millenia.

Beachwalking Perhaps the greatest pleasure in walking a beach is the solitude you experience, whether you are truly by yourself or are with a few friends. It is not loneliness, but a "splendid isolation" that separates you from the rest of the world and returns you to the natural—even primeval—earth. Waves rolling in crashing rhythm surge upon the beach, receding in bubbling form as they did before life existed on this planet. Whistling, rustling wind and surf grow lulling and hypnotic. You walk or lie on the beach, as the cares of the world ebb away and a tired and taut body relaxes. Nothing really matters here.

It makes little difference whether you are on the beach in the heat of a midsummer noonday sun, on the darkest of moonless nights, or in the cold blasts of winter. Winter beach walking is not a popular pastime: it requires determination as well as thermally efficient clothing; but this may be a time when the beach is its most beautiful and you are most isolated from the busy world. A sharp eye will tell you that you are not completely alone; other life is present. Far beyond the surf on the cold, iron-gray water, dark rafts of sea ducks cluster together, rising and falling in the long swells of winter. Behind you, in the distance, a few ponies cross the barrier dune on their way into the shelter of thicket and pine forest.

Beachwalking is especially memorable when fog rolling in great banks pushes across the dulled and quieted water, covers the beach, penetrates the island with vaporous tendrils, and finally curtains the tall pines from sight. In the fog your very existence, your whole world, is narrowed to a brief hemisphere of perception that dissolves into nothingness. It is as though you were the only person in the world, walking upon pristine sands that bear no tread of any living creature, leaving behind footprints that as surely as the tide rises will soon be erased forever.

Still a different kind of day that lures you to the beach is the day of a northeaster, a gusty, rain-laden day with low, dark clouds scudding overhead. Now you walk the upper beach, well away from the crashing waves. Your senses respond to the moaning wind, to booming surf, to spume flung airborne from the crest of each tall wave as it breaks, creating sheets of salt mist that encrust your face and clothes. Experience such a storm but once, and it will remain with you for a lifetime. Years later, in reverie, you will take again that solitary walk buffeted by sand-laden wind along the coast of Assateague in the face of a great storm.

The smells of the sea attract. They are quite apart from the smells we normally experience. I know of no sea odor that has ever repelled me. Great rafts of seaweed cast into the wrack zone, dead and decaying conchs or horseshoe crabs stranded by storm waves: their odors may be strong, but overall there still is a sea fragrance that draws us back to the water's edge again and again.

A side benefit of beachwalking belongs to the collector. Real treasures cast up by the waves are exciting to dream about, whether or not ever realized. What is it that will be carried in by the tide? Most jetsam is trivia with little monetary value; but cherished bits of driftwood, an old scoured bottle, a cork float from a seine net, or remnants of marine lives that have been disturbed from the sea floor and thrown up to dry in the beach wrack are in themselves a form of treasure. Rare is the beachwalker who does not return to his car or home without pockets full of pebbles, shells, bits of rounded colored glass, smoothed wood—small, inconsequential, but irresistible things that years later, lying on a shelf, will recall that day.

Who knows what it is that pulls us back to the seashore, or lures us from far inland when we have never even seen the ocean? Some might say it is a deep-seated, instinctive tugging to the edge of the deep where our ancestral lives began eons ago. Hardly this—but I believe that the clean salt air, the constant breeze, the rhythmic surf, all combine to form an environment that country or city dwellers do not normally experience, and one that we must seek out.

Truly one of the most profound effects of beach-walking is the way in which long and troubled thoughts vanish in the sea breeze. Suddenly you have walked a considerable distance without once being ensnared by cares so shortly left behind. Your mind is washed as clean as the sand. I clearly recall early boyhood walks along very different shores half a world away from Assateague, half a century ago. Those distant beaches—what I saw on them, how they felt, how they sounded, their distinctive odors—are as vivid today as the day I walked upon them. By now I have walked beaches over much of the world: I can pull out a map and point to one spot or another, on some continent or a tiny mid-oceanic island, and immediately be there. Somehow I do not experience the same completeness of recollection for other places that I do for the shore. Your trips to Assateague can be as memorable.

A violent storm in 1962 left boats in the streets and yards of Chincoteague. It wrecked most development on Assateague Island and so reopened the issue of making it a national seashore.

Barrier to the Sea Barrier islands are found throughout the world, forming much of the East Coast of the United States and a little less than 10 percent of all global shorelines. Each runs parallel to a sandy coastline, separated by a bay that may be 2 to 12 kilometers (1 to 8 miles) wide. A barrier island itself is not broad, perhaps as little as 50 meters (160 feet) or as much as a kilometer (one-half mile). Assateague Island at the moment is approximately 60 kilometers (37 miles) long; but it has not been that in the past, nor will it necessarily be so in the future.

Barrier islands never occur off shores that plunge directly into the depths, as along our West Coast. Instead they are products of the dynamics of both a coastal plain and a continental shelf, which are actually one continuous slope of sedimentary deposits with a temporary dividing line created by a sea level that rises and falls through geological time. The whole exposed plain and submerged shelf system is approximately 500 kilometers (300 miles) broad along much of the Atlantic Coast, the submerged continental shelf at present extending from the shoreline nearly 80 kilometers (50 miles) before dropping sharply eastward toward the sea floor hundreds of meters deep. To the west, the sudden rise of the rocky Piedmont uplands marks the inland edge of the coastal plain and the original, prehistoric shoreline. During times when much of the world's water was locked up in huge glaciers, the sea level was many meters below what it is now and many kilometers out to the east, with great rivers running across the wide plain cutting canyons that today regularly notch the submerged edge of the continental shelf. The closest canyon to Assateague on the south is Washington Canyon, 70 kilometers (45 miles) from Chincoteague, while Baltimore Canyon is many kilometers north of Ocean City inlet.

It is difficult to say precisely how old Assateague Island is, for it constantly changes both its position and its composition. It is easily 6,000 years old, but it has moved and evolved over the years, sand replacing sand, so it really is not the same island from age to age.

Have you wondered where the sand of northern beaches comes from, and how it is ground so fine? Sand's origin is in the distant geological past, when enormous rivers carried water melted from the glaciers across the rocky land to the sea. The glaciers, as much as 1.5 kilometers (1 mile) high, ground rocks beneath their crushing weight, but it was primarily the action of water, scouring rock against rock, that pulverized them into such fine particles. The smaller they were, the more easily they were carried downstream in the swift rivers, until they reached the ocean where the flowing currents lost their velocity. Near river mouths sand and sediment dropped down to carpet the near-shore and in this fashion a thick mantle, about 1.5 kilometers (1 mile) deep and composed of many distinct layers, was gradually built into the continental shelf. Each layer displays clear evidence of the advance and retreat of great continental ice sheets.

Because there were several distinct Ice Ages, each separated by thousands of years, it is certain that sealevel fluctuations created widely different conditions at one time or another. For example, sea level was lowest about 15,000 years ago when ice locked up so much water that the ocean, by various estimates, was from 75 to 135 meters (250 to 450 feet) lower than it is today. At other times, it was

Next two pages: The power of waves lies in their relentless persistence. When driven by great storms, the impact to the shore is dramatic. Intense northeaster storms, in 1992 and 1998, greatly altered Assateague's beach, most notably a few miles south of the Ocean City inlet near the northern end and on Toms Cove Hook at the southern end.

Beach wrack creates endless mosaics and collages up and down the ocean beach. Pebbles tumbled smoothe as gemstones, seashells sanded down to their alabaster interiors, bits of bird feathers . . . all become materials of ephemeral artwork your eye or camera can frame and capture forever. Water-sculpted sand (opposite) looks like a working model of the eroded topography of the Southwest.

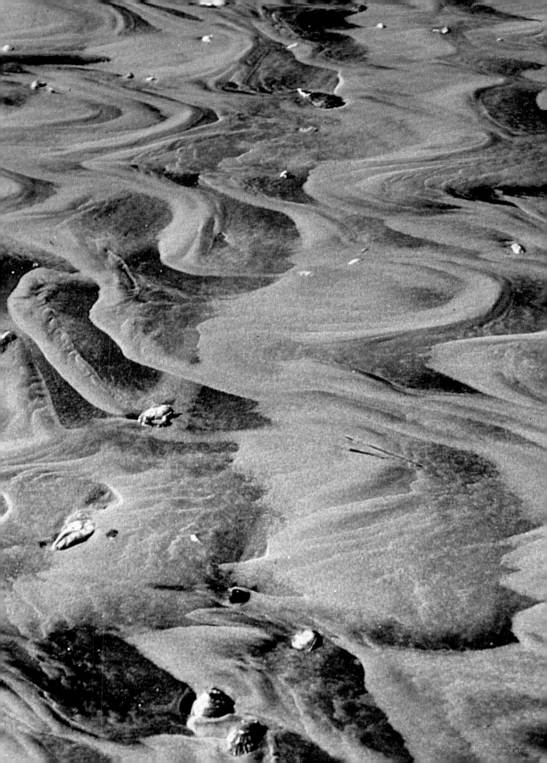

at least 7 meters (25 feet) higher than it is now; but the record may be broken, for ours is an age of rising seas with no immediate end in sight. The level of the ocean rose quite rapidly until 5,000 years ago, then slowed, and now rises about 30 centimeters (12 inches) every century. This doesn't sound like much; but you must remember that the sandy shore of a coastal plain is only gently sloped, so a few centimeters' difference in sea level can mean a considerable invasion of water across a low-lying shore.

So it is that marine fossils are found well inland upon the coastal plain today, while at the same time we may dredge up old tree trunks complete with roots a half-kilometer (one-third mile) offshore. The actual shoreline has wandered back and forth obeying forces of a sinking or a rising coastline and a lowered or elevated sea level, all the while following the dictates of coastal currents. Islands lying just offshore, products of these coastal forces, surely have been immersed or raised from the sea on numerous occasions. Such barrier islands, composed entirely of sand, owe their very existence to the great worldwide fluctuations of climate that four times spelled drastic changes for our planet earth.

If individual sand particles could be traced, we would find that Assateague is composed of rock fragments from far inland, perhaps even from the northern center of the continent. Certainly the Appalachians have contributed much to its presence.

Should you take a submarine ride across the continental shelf, you would find a series of sand ridges lying more or less parallel to the present shoreline. Probably these are ancient drowned barrier islands, although some may have been sand bars that never broke the surface. Old sea levels that remained in place long enough to cut wave terraces on the shelf and plain are still to be found. There are at least seven of them, and each has its ridges thrown up by storm waves that may have surfaced to form barrier islands in the past. If remnants of terrestrial vegetation, including salt marsh peat, can be dredged from their inner or western sides, we know that they once emerged. But if they ever were real islands, they are now well-hidden beneath the Atlantic.

Even a modern barrier island such as Assateague resembles an iceberg: 99 percent of its mass and structure is hidden from view beneath the surface.

We see only dry shifting sands or darker areas where vegetation has taken hold, but deep beneath our feet is a complex assortment of sands, clays, and other sediments, each laid down by the work of sea currents and waves that ground and sorted out particles according to their weight and size. Whenever a wave begins to lose force, particles it has carried drop to the bottom, large ones or heavier minerals first, smaller ones or lighter minerals later. When storm waves arrive in strength, then even large rock fragments are once again moved and even suspended briefly in the turbulent water. As we shall see, seasonal differences in wave strength have a profound effect upon beach shape.

Traveling Sands Over thousands of years the broad, wave-cut plains of glacial sediment have always given way when confronted by waves and currents of the sea. Sands that emerge above surface shift constantly and remain in the vicinity only because of the binding action of vegetation, especially that of a salt marsh. For any barrier island, the principal and immediate source of sand is from offshore, usually from submerged bars, which are subject to the most erosion by waves in shallow water. Sand bars themselves are moved about, built up rapidly, or destroyed almost overnight. Because of their uncertain location and height, they have been threats to mariners as long as man has sailed the seas. It is impossible to chart them permanently, but over the long run sand from bars, transported by waves and currents, moves shoreward into even more dynamic beach areas. There sand particles not only continue to be subject to the forces of water movement, but for the first time are transported by strong onshore winds.

Barrier island sand may be carried back to the sea, moved along the beach, piled up in large dunes, or carried across the island by wind or by storm overwash to be dropped into the quiet bay on the other side. Once in the bay, sand is soon covered by vegetation and mud, and does not reappear until the island has moved to such an extent that it is again exposed to the sea.

To the casual beach visitor, it is clear that currents traveling more or less parallel to the shore—longshore, or littoral, currents—are major agents for the

transport of sand. It is equally obvious that waves, especially powerful storm-generated ones, are opaque with suspended sediment and create drastic alterations of beach form. If you visit the shore in both summer and winter, you will notice major seasonal differences in the width and slope of beaches.

The origin of most Atlantic barrier islands, Assateague in particular, is the result of several major events, each depending upon others to create a long, sandy island. First, there is the possibility that some barrier islands are isolated primary dunes, cut off from the land behind them as the sea level rose, or as storms washed out large areas to their rear. Then there are the offshore sand ridges mentioned earlier, either newly created ones or remnants of old submerged bars or even of prehistoric islands.

Without question, the sandy sediment from which barrier islands are built is normally provided by offshore areas. This sand is worked gradually toward the shore by waves and currents, at times being thrust up to emerge from the sea as a sandy island off the main beach with a long shallow strip of quiet water in between. It seems, though, that the major barrier islands, of which Assateague is one, grew most rapidly as a result of an additional event.

A herring gull patrols the stormy beach against a backdrop of murky surf. Camouflaged against foraging predators, the eggs of a skimmer rest in a simple scrape in the sand.

One of the major features of sedimentary shorelines such as we have along the Atlantic Coast is the presence of hooked capes. Cape Cod is a very large one, but along the entire coast are smaller examples, each of which is growing outward, curving back upon itself, eventually closing the gap to become a rounded promontory. Assateague was once the southern tip of a peninsula that grew southeast from Delaware, extended by littoral currents carrying sand along the shore face. More than 50 kilometers (30 miles) of such growth has already occurred, and the extension continues. Between 1924 and 1970, the hook at the southern end of the island, near Chincoteague, lengthened by three kilometers (two miles). A lighthouse, a fish factory, a Coast Guard station, and oystering in Toms Cove have all been made obsolete by siltation in the cove.

While barrier islands often originate from already-existing spits, the sediments of which they are composed are brought in from the shallow continental shelf. Together these forces create islands, extend and alter spits, curve peninsulas into hooks, and nibble away at other shoreline areas until erosion becomes a major problem to man's plans for development of the coastline. The velocity and strength of currents, both offshore and littoral, have a sorting and winnowing effect upon marine sediments. Heavier rock particles are left behind at sea, while sand is arranged in layers along the shore and on beaches according to its density and particle size. For this reason, even in one short stretch of beach, sand varies markedly in its composition.

Not only do barrier islands extend lengthwise along the main continental shoreline, but they also migrate toward the mainland as the sea rises or the coastal plain submerges under the weight of its accumulated sediments. The northern portion of Assateague Island has moved more than 300 meters (1,000 feet) to the west in the last 30 years, primarily because jetties were constructed to keep the Ocean City inlet open. After storms, when whole "forests" are exposed on the eastern beach, there is ample evidence that the entire island is on the move toward the continent across the bay. Although we notice some change from time to time, especially when jetties or other manmade structures interfere with current patterns, a lifetime usually is not long enough to see the overall trend. But old maps and charts, made accurately a century and more ago, clearly show what changes are taking place. For example, today at the southern tip of Assateague, near Chincoteague, the water is shallower offshore than at the northern end, with waves breaking over bars much farther out. Because waves arrive obliquely upon the shore, littoral or 'longshore currents are stronger at the southern end and the water is very turbid from sand and sediment in suspension. Underwater visibility is poor close to any barrier island: at Assateague it is limited to one meter or less near the southern portion and only a little more toward the northern end.

In short, barrier islands are the result of water movement, coastal erosion, and a rise in sea level as the marine environment invades the land. The remarkable thing is that, delicate as these islands seem to be, they persist and are always present no matter how they alter form and position over the ages. They are true manifestations of natural forces that we can do little either to stop or to encourage.

Assateague Island, dynamic and interesting, is typical youthful shoreline.

The Changing Shore Anyone visiting a seashore soon becomes aware of tides and variations in wind velocity. High tides occur along the Atlantic coast twice a day, but there is a monthly cycle as well. When both the Moon and the Sun exert their gravitational pull on the fluid mass of water encircling the Earth, tides rise exceptionally high and fall exceptionally low; these are known as spring tides. When the Sun and the Moon are at right angles to one another with respect to the Earth, there is a smaller rise and fall of the tides; these are called neap tides.

When a spring tide coincides with a strong onshore wind, masses of water pile up on the beach, and if there is a low point in the primary dune they flood over into the low, flat areas behind. This tidal overwash not only has a major physical effect upon the island by transporting sand along with the flow but severely affects all life occurring in its path. It may also carry along hapless marine organisms caught in the surge, depositing them far from their normal habitat. An overwash pool may contain a variety of marine plants and animals still alive in the warmed, slowly sinking water. Some animals, such as the tube-dwelling shrimp, may construct a new burrow. But such life is doomed, for the water percolates down through the sand, leaving creatures from the sea dying either in the increasing dryness or in the fresh water that lies not far below the surface—conditions they cannot tolerate even briefly.

Dune plants in the way of an overwash either are immediately affected by the high salt content and die or, if they have the proper adaptations, may be tolerant enough to survive the briefly hazardous condition.

Should a washover be extensive enough, it may reach the far side of the island, dumping large quantities of sand into the open bay or on the salt marsh. This effectively widens the island, although it may temporarily destroy the marsh. Salt-marsh cordgrass soon invades the new deposits, however; and the island will have grown into the bay and moved toward the continent a little more. Good examples of overwash areas are found in Big and Little Fox Lev-

A red fox traverses the inland shore of Toms Cove. Beyond the oyster watch house the primary dune forms your horizon, blocking the view of the ocean.

Harbor seals occasionally turn up as far south as Assateague. This small seal inhabits north Atlantic coasts and sometimes ascends rivers.

A closer look at the harbor seal reveals its streamlined adaptations for mobility and retention of body heat in cold ocean waters.

els and Wash Flats. Overwash, despite attempts by humans to prevent it, is a highly constructive process and perfectly natural on a barrier island. When we try to prevent overwash to protect our resort homes and coastal industries, we become a far worse enemy to the permanence of a barrier island than the sea and wind to which the island conforms in an ever-changing equilibrium, giving a little and taking a little. Man's efforts lead to inevitable breakdown of that equilibrium, eventually with grievous results not only to his interests but to the entire island system. Whatever he does along a sandy coast is doomed to failure so long as he attempts to contend with the natural forces of the sea.

Storms coupled with high tides perform another natural function that man also views with alarm and usually considers a catastrophic event. If the surging masses of water rising upon a beach find a relatively narrow, weak spot in the primary dune, there is an enormous inrush of water that carves out a new inlet where none existed before. Studies of Assateague have shown that inlet formation, as well as the closing of old inlets, has occurred regularly through the ages and with some frequency even in recent times. There have been at least 11 navigable inlets through Assateague Island since records have been kept, and many more smaller ones. Finally, in 1933 Assateague was severed from the mainland, of which it had been a long peninsula, and became a separate island. This hurricane-created inlet was found useful and subsequently has been kept open by jetties. Remnants of past inlets, now closed over and filled in, may be found in the vicinity of Sandy Point, Green Run, Sugar Point Cove, Winter Quarter Gut, Fox Hill Levels, Slough Inlet, Pope Island, and Toms Cove. Even the heavily used Chincoteague Inlet is now so narrow that tidal exchange from bay to sea is swift and forceful, with currents scouring the channel to depths of ten meters (32 feet) and more. As it widens, apparently the trend at present, the water will become shallower and not so easily navigated, although there is nothing certain about predicting its future. Ocean City Inlet, opened by the hurricane of 1933, probably would have closed long ago were it not for the jetties and dredging. It appears to be one of the few breaches in Assateague that man has welcomed, although it is now expensive to maintain.

How long this inlet will remain usable or even possible to retain is a question that cannot be answered, for its jetties have interrupted the 'longshore drift in such a fashion as to invoke potential erosion of the beach fronting Ocean City itself.

Sooner or later, a natural inlet is going to be closed by littoral currents swirling along the shore. When inlets close and access to the sea is denied, a bay behind an island becomes brackish with freshwater from intermittent rain and tributary streams, and the life it contains alters accordingly. If an inlet remains in place for many years, a tidal delta usually develops from sand and silt deposited by incoming tides. Such a delta is soon stabilized by mats of algae and later by rooted aquatic plants, until the whole accumulation rises as salt marsh to the level of the high tide. At this point, the newly emerged land is stable and will not easily wash away, since tidal flow now follows a network of channels or sloughs through the marshy delta.

Storms and hurricanes cause the most dramatic changes to a barrier island. Even though they occur infrequently, they cause profound alterations. Enormous loss of sand is seen in one area, with substantial deposition in another. Inlets are ripped open in a matter of hours; and the sloping beach, or berm, is stripped away until it grows narrow, leaving a steep face rising to the primary dune—if the dune still remains. These same storm waves build offshore bars parallel to the shore and wash thousands of tons of sand over the island into the bay. After such storms ancient wrecks may be uncovered, their dark keels and ribs emerging in stark contrast to the light sand. Sometimes a whole forest of cedar or pine stumps is revealed on the ocean side of an eroded berm, perhaps only for a short period until the littoral drift covers them again with sand from elsewhere along the shore. In the dirty water following a storm, large rounded chunks of old marsh peat, still held together by ancient marsh grass stems and roots, roll about in the subsiding surf and are often cast upon the shore. These peat rollers are commonly seen along the Assateague shore, but most visitors take them to be of recent origin, from present-day marshes, rather than relics that have lain buried beneath the island for centuries as it moved slowly landward over them. Only when a storm removes sand are the old marsh beds exposed and chunks broken off to be tossed about in the surf.

A Migrating Island When a barrier island first forms, it is vulnerable not only to great storms but also to ordinary marine forces of wind, waves, currents, and tides. Its height builds slowly until it eventually reaches an average elevation of about 1.5 meters (5 feet), at which point it is usually stabilized by plants.

New barrier islands shift continually because of their fine, loose soil, which at first is nothing more than pure sand, nearly white with a high quartz content. Later, as plants take hold and then decay, leaving organic residues, the sand grows gray and dark with accumulated debris, its particles bound together by silt and organic matter. Toward the rear of the island, back in the area of thickets and secondary dunes where stands of loblolly pine grow, soil has become a sandy loam near the surface. It supports a greater variety of vegetation than in the interdune area or in the high dunes close to the beach. If you should examine sands from the beach all the way back to the bay, you would find a gradual decrease in particle size, for the most common agent of transport of sand grains is the wind, and the larger particles are not so easily blown or rolled along. In the event of severe storms or powerful overwash, everything is moved en masse regardless of the size of individual grains.

All barrier island soils, with the exception of dense marsh muds on the bay side, are loose enough to allow water to sink quickly through the surface layers until it reaches the water table that lies a meter or so beneath. Normally this water table is fresh and can be seen emerging into depressions in the interdune region to form freshwater marshes or even small ponds. At times, however, during overwash in the flats, enough saltwater percolates down to make the water table slightly saline for a while; but this soon dissipates and the freshwater condition is restored. Water, whether salt from storm overwash or fresh from heavy rain, seldom stays on the surface of a barrier island very long. When pools are apparent, you may be sure they are the water table itself. But where dunes build to heights of three to five meters (10–15 feet)—or even, as on the bay side at the southern end of Assateague Island, to 15 meters (48 feet)—the water table is well out of reach.

Dunes, no matter what their height, grow as a result of an obstruction to sand-carrying wind. It makes no difference what the barrier is: a plant, a bit of driftwood, a snow fence. Sand accumulates in the lee and the accumulation grows both in height and in length. The lee of such an obstruction is known as a wind shadow, and normally you can see a long, elevated streamer of sand behind even such a small object as a seashell or a pebble brought in by the waves.

A barrier island is the product not just of the sea and an occasional violent storm, but of the average climatic conditions of the region. The ocean moderates coastal climate with its constant water temperature, eliminating extremes of heat or cold and encouraging an even amount of rainfall throughout the year, with the driest periods occurring in the autumn. Prevailing winds, coming from the northeast and southeast, bring with them a variety of mineral compounds from the sea: salts of calcium, sodium, potassium, and magnesium. These salts profoundly affect life on a barrier island, especially plants and the few animals that live near the primary dune. The maritime influence of salt spray diminishes across the island until, on the bay side, it is almost absent. Even close to the sea, its effect may be minimized if it is accompanied by heavy rain that washes it from plant stems into the sand.

One of the features that attracts people to Assateague is the cool ocean air in summer, with temperature averaging a comfortable 20°C (68°F) near the water. In midwinter the island is cold and windy, but the actual temperature is fairly moderate. Because of the moderate temperatures summer or winter, the high humidity due to sea winds is seldom uncomfortable.

Extremes in weather are remembered for years by those who experience them. The Great Hurricane of 1933, before hurricanes were given names, wreaked havoc along the Atlantic Coast. Hazel in 1954 and both Connie and Diane in 1955 did major damage; and the severe storm of March 1962, although not a hurricane, affected the island as much as many past hurricanes. But great storms are a fact of barrier-island existence and are ever-possible hazards to

Next two pages: Stabilized by grasses, a primary dune holds its own close to the surf's reach. Scenes like this are the stuff of beachwalking.

development. These seemingly fragile islands give way in the face of violent storms, only to recover quickly afterward.

So Assateague, one of the great barrier islands of our Atlantic Coast, continues to be on the move, as it has been for thousands of years. It grows in length. It is severed into fragments as new inlets form. It marches inexorably toward the continent across the bay—a water gap that will, however, continue to exist as long as the sea level rises and slowly inundates the coastal plain.

The Restless Waves One of the first features of island shores to which we are drawn is the surf. The ever-changing pattern of waves, breaking offshore and flooding up the beach only to wash back in frothy sheets to the sea again, is a soothing and hypnotic sight.

Waves seldom approach a shoreline head-on, but generally attack it obliquely. This angled procession of waves creates the littoral currents that move sand along a beach like a conveyor belt and, in a complex fashion still not thoroughly understood, scallop the waterline into cusps at regular intervals. Cusps are low mounds of beach material separated by crescent-shaped troughs, with fine-grained layers of sand in the "bays" and thicker layers of coarser sand making up the "headlands."

The gentle waves of summer build a beach or berm until it is wide and almost flat, or with only a slight incline. "Ordinary" storms also build beaches, but the major ones, with waves a meter or more above the normal tide level, wash away great quantities of sand, or thrust it inland over the island to deposit it in the bay where the transporting waves finally lose their force.

Because waves usually approach a beach at an angle, setting up littoral or 'longshore currents, the water moved along the face of a beach must eventually go somewhere. Every so often it will gather into a major flow-out across a low point in an offshore sandbar and rush seaward. This is known as a rip current and is thought by many swimmers to be an "undertow" that carries them dangerously out to sea. A true undertow is seldom powerful or hazardous; it is simply a slipping of water washing back into the sea, along the bottom, after it has penetrated as far up a beach as wave force will allow. It may tug a little, but is hardly enough to sweep you off your feet. A rip current is another matter. But there is no reason for panic if a swimmer finds himself caught in one. While it is almost impossible to swim back to shore *through* such a powerful current, a simple way of escaping is merely to swim parallel to the shore. Rip currents are not wide and soon a swimmer finds himself in quiet water where he can turn and return to the beach without difficulty. Seen from a distance, a rip current is obvious enough, not so much from surface turbulence as from discoloration, for this current is about the only means by which beach sediment can be carried out to sea across the offshore sandbars.

In winter, with increased winds and forceful waves, a beach is cut away, narrowing the berm and even creating a small, steep cliff face, or scarp, up against the primary dune. Small scarps are sometimes seen in summer if waves attack a beach at a very sharp angle, creating an excessive littoral current; but they are not common then.

When great storms arrive, summer or winter, wave patterns are no longer predictable, and the whole marine topography is wild and disordered, with waves attacking the shore from every possible angle. Occasional pulses of waves can be seen in storms, building pressure every now and then until huge masses of water rise up and flood over or through the barrier dune to rush in heavy sheets across the intertidal flats. The force of such water movement, carrying thousands of tons of sand, is stupendous.

After a storm subsides, all we can do is marvel at the awesome power of water in motion. In a short span of hours, the entire beach, dune, and inland topography may be altered beyond recognition, yet a year later the inexorable processes of reconstruction, both physical and by vegetation, have done their work and all seems familiar and normal again, even if the scenery is not precisely what it had been before.

The rushing swash and lesser backwash of each wave on a beach face is a never-ending source of fascination. The thin sheet of water, fringed by foam, climbs the face as far as wave energy can take it, slows to a halt while its forward margin sinks into the sand and the remaining water slides back down the slope. Near the point of greatest penetration are multitudes of dimples, holes, and small domes in the wet sand. These surface features are not the work of animals beneath the sand, as you might suspect, but of trapped air that causes minor disturbances among the loose particles when it escapes from the saturated sand.

Just below where the swash first rushes up the slope, in the region slightly beyond the water line, lies a shallow trough bounded a few meters farther seaward by a small, temporary sand bar. Often the beach side of the trough is quite abrupt, so a wader stepping out into the water suddenly plunges 15 or 20 centimeters (6 or 8 inches) into loose, coarse sand that is rattled about by wave action. This 'longshore trough, while a temporary and constantly changing feature, may harbor a number of living things that are able to contend with the hazards of rolling water and suspended abrasive sand particles. Often there are small fishes here, darting about, spending a great amount of energy simply maintaining themselves in the turbulent situation. Here too are swimming crabs, especially the red-spotted lady crab, and small hermit crabs in their snail-shell homes. But all these creatures do better outside of the temporary 'longshore bar where the water is quieter, where the roller action of normal waves does not reach so deep, and where the sand is finer and not disturbed so much.

The littoral current is not only an excavator and a conveyor of sand along the shore. It also serves for the dispersal of larval life forms, such as those of the ghost crab and mole crab. Nearly all marine animals have free-swimming or planktonic larval beginnings, often carried at the mercy of currents, so a shoreline receives continuous arrivals of new lives that repopulate beaches destroyed by storms. Of course, most larvae perish at sea, being eaten by predators or succumbing to a host of other environmental hazards; but there are always sufficient numbers left to assure survival of each species.

Sometimes, after a major storm, sand may build up on the lower beach to form a long dike behind which a lake of sea water is trapped. This is a profitable place to observe marine life, similar to the more common tide pools of rocky shores. Usually the life trapped in such beach pools is doomed because, as the water warms in the sun, it not only evaporates but also loses its dissolved oxygen. Occasionally the lives caught here are saved when a high tide breaks through and flushes out the pool. Similar but much more temporary pools may be formed if the 'longshore bar just outside the trough breaks the surface, briefly isolating the trough from the sea until the tide floods back in. When such a pool forms, it is true tide pool; but unlike those of rocky coasts, it cannot be counted on to reappear with every low tide.

What is trapped in these temporary pools? Small shoreline fishes, including silversides and anchovies, various molluscs, sand shrimp, hermit crabs, and burrowing worms are good possibilities. Because these creatures are confined here with no chance of escape until the tide comes in again, a beach pool is a favorite feeding ground for shorebirds.

Sea water does not penetrate far back into the sand of a beach where the water table becomes fresher from rain trapped in the island sediments. But living in the wet sand of the lower beach, deep down among the sand grains, are organisms seldom seen by people. Their obscurity is due mostly to their microscopic size, although occasionally on sunny days some varieties of single-celled organisms congregate in such numbers close to the surface that they color the sand yellowish or greenish. They are photosynthetic "plant-animals" of a sort that require sunlight and moisture, but not the open sea, for their life activities. With darkness and incoming tides, they sink to the safety of lower levels in the sand.

On a dark and moonless night, other near-microscopic creatures are apparent to the beach-walker. As you cross wet sand where the tide recedes, you may find with every step hundreds of ghostly pinpricks of bright light radiating outwards from the pressure of each footprint. If you hop up and down, the radius increases dramatically, until a large area shines momentarily. The animals causing this phenomenon are often small marine crustaceans, a type of amphipod shrimp, although at times, if the sand is wet enough, the luminescence may be produced by single-celled protozoans known as *Noctiluca scintillans,* or "shining light-of-the-night." At times these tiny, apple-shaped flagellates are so abundant in the water that they cause breaking waves to be outlined in a cold, fiery glow.

Life from Shore to Forest

Where waves break upon the shore, only a few kinds of highly specialized animals are able to exist. Best known is the ovoid, streamlined mole crab about the size and shape of your end thumb joint. This remarkable little crustacean rides in, swimming, with the wave swash. Then, by means of highly developed appendages and a triangular terminal portion of its abdomen, it quickly burrows into the sand, facing the beach. Once in place, it raises a pair of eyes located at the end of long stalks and unfolds two sets of antennae. When closely pressed together, one pair of antennae forms a breathing tube or snorkel, while the other much larger pair is feathery and is held in the backwash of a wave, straining out bits of organic matter carried down from the beach. Mole crabs change their position constantly. At times swarms of them can be seen darting about in water only centimeters deep as the wave washes onto the beach, only to disappear almost immediately beneath the sand as the sheet of water races back down the beach face. At other times, a beach may be truly devoid of mole crabs, perhaps for a kilometer or more. And when a wader is nipped on the toe by a lady or calico crab, it may be that the crab reached out to grab what appeared to be a particularly large and plump mole crab!

A very different animal living in somewhat the same way is *Donax,* a tiny, brightly colored bivalve popularly known as a bean clam. Because of predators, parasites, and environmental factors, its populations fluctuate widely. But when it occurs in huge numbers, the entire beach seems to twinkle and glisten with the clams' burrowing activities, as waves rush in and subside into the sand. Bean clams, like the mole crabs, strain minute particles of food from the recurring rush of waves.

A great variety of animals lives farther up the beach. Some of them are terrestrial in origin, but most are of marine ancestry. In the jumbled beach wrack thrown up by waves may be a whole association of small creatures, mostly insects such as beetles, ants, and fly larvae, as well as occasional spiders, myriapods, and crustaceans.

The crustacean most common to this zone and higher on the berm, is known as a beach flea. Not an insect at all, it is better called a beach hopper. This amphipod crustacean with large bluish eyes and well-developed jumping legs is omnivorous, feeding on bits of organic debris in the beach wrack and on crumbs of food left by picknickers. It will even sample human bathers drying off in the late afternoon sun. Beach hoppers tend to be more active in twilight and evening hours, as do their much larger cousins of the beach, the swift ghost crabs, whose burrows are seen in daytime but whose actual presence usually has to be confirmed after dark. The safest way to approach a ghost crab and see it clearly is to go out at night with a powerful flashlight: when the beam is directed on the crab it usually pauses in its activities, blinded by the light, not sure of direction or of your movement. Should a ghost crab emerge in daylight and you are able to watch it for a while, you will see it feed on all sorts of organic matter littering the beach. The crab may even bury large objects such as dead fish for a later food supply. Ghost crab claws are powerful and not only can cut off bits of flesh or plant material and shred them before eating, but can give a careless human a painful nip when the animal is captured and picked up. Capturing one is difficult, though, for a ghost crab on land is one of the swiftest crabs in the world.

A ghost crab is essentially a land-dwelling animal; but it is of marine ancestry, as proved by its need to return to the surf zone to release its eggs, which then hatch and proceed through various stages of planktonic larval development almost indistinguishable from those of other sea crabs. The ghost crab is a remarkable land animal in that it has retained gills; but these are much increased in surface area and must be kept moist to allow for an adequate exchange of oxygen and carbon dioxide between their blood and the air. Providing the crab can keep its gills moist by remaining in deep burrows during hot days, it is able to live not only high on the berm but even well inland over the primary dune, 90 meters (100 yards) or more away from the sea. It can go for two days without re-wetting its gills at all, quite an achievement for an animal with an aquatic past that, in an evolutionary sense, is very recent.

Normally a sandy beach is a formidable obstacle

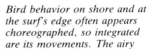

Bird behavior on shore and at the surf's edge often appears choreographed, so integrated are its movements. The airy agility of piping plover (top left), sandpiper (bottom left), and common tern (top right) carries over to their feeding habits on shore. Here a tern makes a food offering in the birds' mating ritual. Laughing gulls, photographically frozen in mid-flight, display varied wing postures. These eastern gulls sometimes show up in the West but do not regularly breed there.

to animals from the sea. Actual invasion of the land in bygone ages occurred not here but far inland in brackish estuaries and freshwater swamps. It is possible that not a single form of animal life, and perhaps not even any plants, ever made a successful transition directly to land by way of a sea beach, even in the more than three billion years that life in some form has existed on this planet, which is itself about four-and-a-half billion years old.

The berm of a beach and the shoreline proper are favorite congregating and feeding places for a wide variety of shorebirds. At dusk on summer evenings, just beyond the breaking waves, you may see black skimmers with their outthrust lower bills cutting the water in search of small fish, leaving widening ripples behind. On the sand, following the swash and backwash, sandpipers and plovers probe for mole crabs, beach hoppers, bean clams, and worms. Herring gulls and laughing gulls come in to rest or to feed on carrion cast up by the tide. Terns hover in the air just offshore, plunge into the water with folded wings, and emerge at once with an anchovy or silversides.

During migration season the wide berm of Assateague has been the feeding and resting place for peregrine falcons whose routes north and south are both inland and out to sea. Probably it is those that follow the coastline that stop off at the barrier island. For many years this swift and uncommon bird was caught without restriction by falconers, thus removing individuals from an already too small breeding population. Fortunately, it is now protected within the area of the national seashore and national wildlife refuge and, at least, on this one island, is no longer in danger of being captured by amateurs.

The beach berm supports only occasional plants, usually such pioneers as seaside-spurge, sea-rocket, and Russian thistle, or saltwort, and these as far from the sea as possible above the reach of extreme high tides. But they are not often present, so the berm for the most part is devoid of living plants.

Dune Wildlife The dunes that rise sharply above the berm are loosely related to, and derived from, the beach. After sand dries in the sun, it is vulnerable to wind action and is moved in sheets or clouds when strong winds blow. Even in light breezes it may slip along the surface. As sand encounters obstacles, such as live vegetation or driftwood and debris deposited by storm tides, the windstream is interrupted and particles drop out in increasing quantities. When sand ridges build, they in themselves become obstacles, so even more sand accumulates upon them. Primary dunes and sand areas inland on the island are composed of very fine sand, for only this is capable of being blown by the wind: the larger grains are left behind on the beach.

Primary dunes are not always continuous along the shore, but may be broken and absent in places where there has been severe overwash. Man comes along, sees such a situation, believes the island needs assistance in rebuilding itself, and erects snow fences or uses some other artificial means of trapping sand. Dunes build quickly and all seems fine until the first great storm arrives and the huge waves it generates find their way blocked as they rise to batter the island. In the long run, overwash and new inlet formation cannot be prevented in the face of such powerful natural forces. The resulting erosion moves enormous quantities of sand that we have been responsible for establishing to new locations, filling bays and blocking channels. The island and our interests inevitably are harmed more than helped by our good intentions.

Where a primary dune has been abruptly eroded by high tides or brisk winds, alternating bands of light and very dark sand create a curious layering effect. The whitish, refractive sand is largely quartz, but the black is magnetite, a heavy mineral nearly three-quarters iron. It originated long ago from eroded, pulverized lava, or possibly from igneous rocks far down in the ocean. The streaking effect is due to sorting action by waves which deposit particles of different weight at different times according to the amount of wave energy available. The origin of most sand, as mentioned earlier, is through the grinding, sorting, and transporting action of rivers, particularly ancient ones that carried meltwater from the retreating glaciers.

A primary or barrier dune is soon naturally stabilized by one of the most ubiquitous of plants: marram, or American beachgrass, grows to the crest of the first dunes and is tolerant of salt spray and blistering summer temperatures. It survives being covered by windblown sand and binds dune slopes together by a knitwork of subsurface horizontal runners, or rhizomes, and by vertical roots that may reach down three meters (nine feet) or more to the water table. Waxy, flexible blades enable it to withstand heat and high winds. Beachgrass is the most important of all dune-stabilizing plants. Once it is established, however, it provides the proper conditions for other salt spray-tolerant plants to take hold. On the lee side of the primary dune you may find another common pioneer, sea-rocket; also some seaside goldenrod, seaside spurge, and sandbur, but never in such abundance as beachgrass.

Primary dunes are visited by animals; even some larger island creatures come here to feed on grass and to hunt one another. Ponies are probably the most obvious vegetarians, but on a lesser scale the maritime locust, a sandcolored grasshopper, is usually present during summer months. Because of its camouflaging coloration, it cannot be seen when it rests on the sand, but when it takes flight, its wings creating a brisk crackling sound, the dark wing color makes the insect obvious until it lands again and seems to disappear.

The temperature of the upper beach and the primary dune is the highest of any land surface on the island. If it is painful for you to run bare-footed over the blistering-hot sand, imagine how it must be for small animals. Most of these, in fact, avoid the surface of the sand in the heat of midday. Some take wing or climb grass stems. Others retreat to burrows or rest in the shade of a plant or under an object, becoming active only when the sun is low or after dark. You can easily determine how the extremes of heat are limited to the immediate surface layer: dig down a few centimeters and you will find relatively cool sand. At night the surface temperature drops; but the sand retains considerable warmth, so that even when the evening breeze is cool you will feel comfortable walking in your bare feet.

In summer, sand temperatures on the primary dune often soar to heights beyond the ability of insects to tolerate, for above approximately 49° C (120° F) insect blood coagulates. A maritime locust has two solutions to this. First, it elevates its body above the surface on six long legs; even a few millimeters of air space between body and hot sand result in some cooling. Second, if it is still too hot, the animal simply takes off and flies to another location or climbs a swaying blade of beachgrass well above the dune's searing temperature. Certain small red-and-blue beetles common to this zone generally escape the extreme temperature of the surface by spending their time running up and down grass blades.

In the vicinity of the primary dune, well beyond the reach of tides, black skimmers and terns nest on the surface in the scant shelter beachgrass provides. Their problem is not to incubate eggs by warming them, but to sit on the nests during daylight hours to keep the eggs shaded and, at least comparatively speaking, cool. It is important that people not disturb birds in nesting areas; for if they are driven from their nests too long or too often, the developing young will die from the heat.

A tern's nest is difficult to see because it is little more than a depression in the sand with mottled, sandcolored eggs lying in the center. After hatching, the chicks, which also resemble the sandy background, crouch motionless as you pass by. The parents warn you, however, with a shrill scolding as they hover above you and then make a swooping attack, which may even include a swift jab on your head as they flash by. They are fearless and the best thing for you to do, both for their young and for your peace of mind, is to leave.

Wind, abrasion by sand, salt spray from the sea, and a deep, almost unavailable water table all combine to make the primary dune a difficult place for plants and animals to live. Only those that can tolerate or adapt to demanding conditions survive.

The Land Beyond Behind the primary dune, in the region of lesser dunes and sand flats, conditions for life are not quite so rigorous. The primary dune shields such areas from the full force of the windborne load of crystalline salt mist, which can be seen billowing in from the sea as a haze across the beach and dissipating rapidly as it nears the dunes. Sand is dropped by all but the strongest winds, so even sizable obstructions in the interdune area do not often build large dunes.

On brisk, windy days when clouds of salt haze drift in from the sea after waves break and throw salt droplets into the air, you may also see dunes "smoke." This is nothing more than sand streaming from dune crests, caught by the wind and blown inland to the interdune region or beyond before descending to add to the sandy surface far removed from the beach proper. Winds of just under 15 kilometers (nine miles) an hour are able to move loose sand, either by rolling it along the surface or by picking it up and carrying it in the airstream.

As you pass the primary dune you may begin to wonder whether the barrier island is the edge of the sea or the edge of the land. It is both. Ecologists recognize a phenomenon known as edge effect, or ecotone; this is a relatively narrow zone bordering two distinctly different environments, such as forest and field. The seashore is the world's most extensive ecotone. An ecotone is more than just a composite of the two environments, since it always has its own characteristics, both physical features and communities of life. Frequently an ecotone may be more populous than its two neighboring regions, although on a sandy beach the transition is too extreme for plants and animals to be as abundant as they are on a rocky coastline with its solid footing. Many organisms found on beaches have become adapted to the sea-land edge and are no longer at home in one parent environment or the other. The ghost crab has permanently forsaken the sea, at least as an adult, while beachgrass cannot live in inland meadows where the soil is rich.

Because high dunes of another sort may rise on the far side of the island near the bay, it is useful to speak of the sandy regions in between as the interdune zone. Actually several distinct habitats are found in the interdune area, but the most common is simply open sand, with small dunelets and hummocks caused by plants that have trapped sand. The region often is extensive, encompassing over half the island's width. The farther one goes from the seaside primary dune, the more stable the sands become, as they grow darker, turning yellow-brown and gray from an accumulation of organic materials.

As you reach the middle of the interdune region you are clearly in the equivalent of a desert zone. The effect of salt spray has diminished, especially if it is accompanied by rain. Temperatures soar and humidity, at least on the sandy surface, is very low.

Life, both plant and animal, not only behaves accordingly, but has structural and functional adaptations to such an environment. Dusty miller, a gray-green plant with a central spikelike cluster of yellow flowers, has leaves that are densely covered with thick white "hairs," or filaments, that serve as an effective dead-air space insulation against the searing rays of the sun. Many dune insects and spiders also are thickly covered with insulating hairlike coats, giving them a furry appearance. Some plants hold their leaves vertically rather than horizontally, an adaptation that not only reduces the amount of sunlight gathered directly, but also the amount of light reflected off the bright sand.

Both the abundance and the variety of plants increase with greater distance from the ocean, resulting in relief from the maritime influence which can so adversely affect intolerant vegetation. As beachgrass and such associates as seaside goldenrod, panic grass, sea rocket, and seabeach evening primrose begin to diminish, a whole new association of plants begins to appear. The plant cover grows more dense, with soft rush, sheep sorrel, sun drops, and dog fennel being common. Yet even well into the interdune region where an occasional dune rises quite high, there may be a reminder of the larger dune close to the sea, for the windward side of such a dune invariably will be knitted together by beachgrass, although on the lee side there may be plants common not only to the interdunes but also characteristic of the thickets beyond: poison-ivy, bayberry, and wax myrtle.

In the interdune region a highly distinctive little plant, *Hudsonia tomentosa,* begins to appear abundantly. It has a variety of common names: poverty-grass, heather, beach-heath, wooly gold-heather. *Hudsonia* is responsible more than any other interdune plant for building dunelets. The tightly bunched, compressed stems, and scale-like, downy leaves trap sand. Invariably every cluster of *Hudsonia* appears elevated on top of a small mound of sand, with a gentle slope of sand streaming out in the lee of the plant. In spring, usually May, these small rounded bunches of beach-heath burst forth in brilliant yellow flowers that carpet the interdune region with unexpected color. Later, the stems and leaves turn a dry-looking grayish green and appear almost dead, although the plant remains very much alive.

Just as vegetation on a barrier island is zoned from sea beach to bay, so are the animals. The whole interdune area is heavily populated by animals, large and small, adapted in different ways to the specialized habitats. Some are dependent upon particular vegetation types. Others suffer from exposure to salt mist or blowing sand and must try to avoid them. Some require specific types of sand and sandy soil in which to live or build burrows.

Ponies are often seen in this semi-protected zone and at times you may see spotted Sika deer, a species of elk introduced from Japan many years ago. They are easily distinguished from the much larger Virginia whitetail deer, which are naturally present. Other native mammals, while not always visible, either live in the interdune area or frequently enter it. They include several kinds of rodents—meadow voles, white-footed or deer mice, and meadow jumping mice. Lapines, represented by the Eastern cottontail, are active all through the region in twilight hours. They are likely prey to the occasional red fox that ventures from its preferred habitat in the thickets and woodlands. Perhaps the most unexpected mammal that hunts in the interdunes at night is the raccoon. It is almost impossible to miss if you go out with a strong flashlight after dark; in daytime, its five-toed tracks pressed into the soft, sandy soil, mark its presence.

The smaller creatures of the interdune area are more abundant than mammals and equally interesting. They are also easier to find during the day. Out in the open sand, frequently close to a stand of grass, you may come across a perfectly round hole plunging straight down. If you touch the edge of the hole, which can be as big around as a finger, you will find that the sand grains around its rim cling together, held in place by silk webbing. Far down at the bottom of the burrow rests a large, sand-colored wolf spider. While it is not in the least dangerous to humans, it is a voracious predator on insects it finds on the surface after dark. If you wish to see one of these spiders without bothering to dig it out, go out at night with a flashlight; wherever greenish pinpoints of light, brilliant as diamonds, shine back at you, there will be a sand wolf spider. You can approach it closely, following the reflections of its eight eyes, to the spot where it straddles the sand, ready to dart off in a flash across the surface in pursuit of prey, which it paralyzes and carries back to its burrow.

Another kind of pit you may come across in the interdune zone, near the thicket area, is a conical depression in the sand excavated by the larva of an antlion. Adult antlions resemble weak and clumsy dragonflies, but the larva is a thick-bodied beast with huge, sickle-shaped hypodermic jaws that inject a tissue-dissolving enzyme into insects it captures. It is the means of preparing for capture that is so interesting. The larva digs its pit by backing around in ever-decreasing circles, flipping sand outward with its broad head. The pit deepens until finally it assumes the shape of a perfect cone, its sides approximately 33 degrees from the vertical, which is the "angle of repose," the steepest slope sand particles can assume without tumbling downhill. The larva buries itself at the bottom and waits for an insect— its prey is not exclusively ants—to blunder into the depression. Once a victim tumbles into the antlion's pit, it finds climbing out almost impossible; every struggling step up the slope brings sand cascading down on top of it. To aid in acquiring a meal, the antlion larva flips sand up and beyond the victim, causing an even greater "landslide." When the insect finally slips to the bottom of the pit, the larva's great curved jaws close on it, the struggles soon cease, and it is carried out of sight beneath the sand.

Many flying insects frequent the interdune zone. Unfortunately they include such pests as greenhead horse flies, deerflies, mosquitoes, and biting midges. There are also agile, "furry" robber flies that, like fighter planes, pursue their victims on the wing. Fortunately, their prey often consist of other insects we find bothersome. The fuzzy, hairy appearance of dune robber flies, so characteristic of many sand-dwelling insects, is another example of how a dense coat of bristles, usually white or light-colored, provides an insulating air space necessary to keep the animal's blood from coagulating in the heat.

Perhaps the most fascinating insects of the interdune region are several species of digger wasps. One in particular, a very small, blue-eyed creature with a black and yellow-banded abdomen, digs like a terrier into the sloping sides of dunes, creating an arched burrow that descends obliquely into the sand.

Next two pages: Many beach and freshwater pond creatures never catch your eye. You might be lucky and see the industrious antlion, or unlucky and get bitten by a greenhead fly or an adult of the mosquito larvae. Some creatures pictured are truly microscopic.

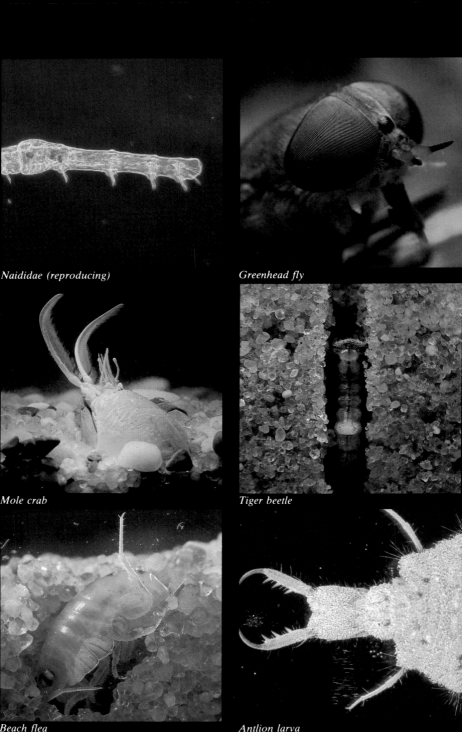

Naididae (reproducing)

Greenhead fly

Mole crab

Tiger beetle

Beach flea

Antlion larva

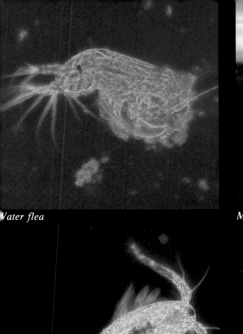

Water flea

Mosquito larvae

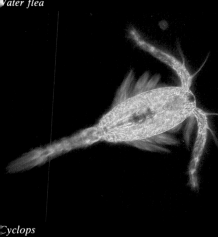

Cyclops

Hydra

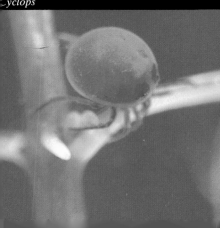

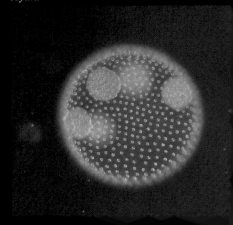

Cardinal flower

Bayberry

Wild grapes

Marsh pink

Old man's beard (lichen)

Rosa rugosa

Beach rose

Rose hips

Saltwort

Thistle

Preceding two pages: Flowers and fruits, ferns, and lichens add color to the prevailing monochromatic sand, grass, and pine needle cover in this area. Wild roses are always a pleasant surprise, as are their seedpod "hips" from which Indians derived vitamin C in winter.

Because these wasps often dig at midday when temperatures are intolerably high—as much as 53° C (129° F) at the surface—they have a behavioral means of preventing a deadly situation from developing. They fly straight up a few centimeters, or even a half-meter (18 inches), hover until they are cool in temperatures that are as much as ten degrees Celsius lower, then descend to dig furiously for a few seconds, then repeat their ascent. Once the burrow is deep enough, the temperature inside is lower and the wasp can work at a more leisurely pace. It provisions each burrow with carcasses of dead and dying insects it finds on the dunes, food for the larval young when they hatch.

The Barren Flats In the normal progression from sea to bay, thickets would follow the interdune region, but on Assateague two other habitats may interrupt this. Where primary dunes have broken down and allowed massive overwash through the interdunes all the way back to the bay itself, there are wide flats nearly barren of life. The flats are kept open because they are low enough to be flooded from the bay with some frequency during high spring tides, especially in winter, so that plants and animals have little chance to become established. On some of the larger flats, sand is thickly bound by clay and is very hard. Animal tracks and wheel ruts hold well in this soil, lasting for more than a year despite periodic washing.

In other areas, flats give way to extensive openings that have a thin, superficial cover of grayish sand. Sometimes multitudes of larval tiger beetles burrow into this yielding, moist sand cover. Their survival in this unpromising habitat is a mystery; a tiger-beetle larva is restricted to its burrow and is fiercely predatory. With its armored, heavily jawed head flush at the sand surface, it waits for prey to come by. When an insect walks near the burrow entrance, the larva pops out like a jack-in-the-box, grabs it, and snaps back in, aided by non-skid bumps on the back of its body as well as by six clawed legs.

But it is rare indeed to find insects walking about the barren flats. With a huge population of tiger beetle larvae in such a restricted zone, it seems likely that all but a few would starve from insufficient food. Although the flats may be periodically flooded by bay water, they are not exposed to the sea again unless there is another severe storm and breakthrough. From the air they appear to be what they undoubtedly are: rather sterile places with little life or color. The only time a tint of color appears in the wide-open spaces is when microscopic, motile one-celled algae rise to the moist surface and lie in the summer sun as they carry on photosynthesis. Then the flats turn greenish-yellow, but other times they are gray.

The only sizable vegetation found on the large flats, as distinct from the small saltmarsh pans, is sparse and exists primarily along the margins. Some saltmarsh cordgrass invades from the bay side, and seabeach orache may burst forth along the edge as well. Spikegrass, beardgrass, and searocket occur only here and there. The overall impression is essentially of a vast area barren of plant life.

Life in the Island Ponds Among the most interesting interruptions to the natural zonation of Assateague are freshwater marshes and small ponds. When you suddenly come across open water toward the rear of the interdune region or in the thicket zone, you are actually witnessing the emergence of the island's water table in a depression. Some of the freshwater marshes wax and wane with the season, at times almost drying up; but the ponds, being somewhat deeper, are more permanent and may last for decades, although no accurate record of them has been kept.

In an ecological sense, Assateague ponds are some of the healthiest of any found along the coastal plain. The reason appears simple enough. On the mainland where farms and settlements depend upon fertilizers and pesticides, open water is affected severely, with many aquatic forms of life either disappearing completely or exploding unnaturally into unbalanced blooms. On Assateague, free from dangerous airborne or waterborne chemicals, the ponds blossom with a rich variety of life, plant and animal. And variety signifies ecological health, whereas large populations of just a few species generally do not.

No other spot on Assateague Island has so many different kinds of plants. More than 60 species are known from these small pockets of freshwater with their surrounding organically enriched and saturated banks. Some, such as water smartweed, water purs-lane, water milfoil, and water pennywort, are true aquatic forms characteristic of ponds anywhere. Water smartweed lies directly in or very close to open water. The others are submerged for all but their seasonal flowering, which is at or above the surface although the leaves of water pennywort may float at the surface. A great many other plants live in the wet soil adjacent to open water. Three-square rush, spikerush, common rush, swamp rose mallow, orache, cattail, and *Phragmites*, or reed grass, are common to such zones; but other less water-oriented plants flourish in the immediate vicinity as well. The one to look for most carefully is poison ivy. You don't have to hunt far because it is one of the commonest plants back in the thickets and woods.

The soil near ponds tends to be acidic, so peat bogs may eventually form after many years. In some pools the water, while transparent, is slightly tea-colored, with the soft, debris-laden brown bottom perfectly visible.

What makes these ponds such a suitable environment for so many organisms? They are well sheltered from maritime winds bearing salt mist: they are partially shaded; they always have enough water; and previous generations of plants that have decomposed have deposited a rich, nourishing organic sediment found nowhere else in the vicinity. The water table of the island, seldom depleted, rises close to the surface, so only a slight depression allows it to be exposed. Just what the origin was of all the deeper ponds is not known, although one deep pond on the Candleberry Trail at North Beach was carved out by water swirling around a house during the 1962 storm. Others may be the result of washouts in past years.

Animals of the island, large and small, are drawn to the ponds and freshwater marshes. The luxuriant vegetation, creating miniature oases, provides both food and shelter. Ponies, deer, and other wild mammals such as raccoons come to drink and feed, while muskrats make their homes there, digging burrows into banks rather than constructing their familiar reed lodges seen on salt marshlands. Otters are known to exist over much of the island's length, although their numbers are not great. Great blue herons, American egrets, and the greater snow goose winter in large numbers in the freshwater marshes, if not in the true ponds, which are too small to support more than a few such large birds.

The expanse of open freshwater naturally provides a suitable place for a number of insect pests to develop, particularly those which have aquatic larval stages, such as mosquitoes (but not the saltmarsh mosquito), horseflies, and midges. But, compensating for these, the ponds also harbor predatory dragonfly nymphs and larval water beetles, as well as predaceous adult beetles, back-swimmers, and water bugs, all of which feed on other aquatic insects. How frogs got to a barrier island such as Assateague across wide expanses of dry sand when it was still a peninsula, or across a saltwater bay which would be lethal to them, is a mystery. Yet frogs are present in the pond and marsh zone, with the southern leopard frog seen and heard frequently. Both tadpoles and adults of this species are present in the pond near Fox Hills. Muskrats are active in this particular pond too, and deer runs go directly to the water's edge. With high secondary dunes providing shelter on the bay side and thickets on the seaward side, island ponds are protected from all but the most severe weather and storm tides. They apparently do not change much from year to year.

All the ponds are rich in microfauna and flora. Geometrically shaped diatoms and desmids, as well as delicate filaments of emerald-green algae, float in the water, but never in such abundance as to indicate organic pollution. All the algae present strongly suggest a healthy, stable condition.

Aquatic animal life is almost beyond reckoning. On the surface are familiar pond insects, including water striders, whirligig beetles, and tiny, primitive springtails that bound across the water film. Closely associated with the surface, rising just long enough to breathe, are several kind of diving beetles, water boatmen, and other air-requiring aquatic insects. Microscopic animal plankton consist of salmon-colored water fleas (cladocerans similar to the familar *Daphnia*); *Cyclops*, bearing twin egg sacs; many kinds of free-swimming rotifers; armored flagellated one-celled organisms; and a variety of protozoans. Some of the latter swim freely, others live in masonry cases on the bottom. Bright green flagellated protozoans swim close to the surface in daylight hours, some elongated and marked with spiral lines, some broad and leafshaped, but all with a single red eye-spot that directs them toward the most intensely lighted areas of the pond.

In the sediment carpeting the pond bottom, elongated copepods and long, slender roundworms wriggle their way through the loose debris. Small segmented worms with a protruding proboscis probe into the soft sediment, retreating quickly downward into burrows when disturbed. Tiny crustaceans and a great many eight-legged water mites crawl or skitter across the dark bottom, either feeding upon dead organic matter or hunting live prey. Green *Hydra* wait, with tentacles outstretched, for passing minute crustaceans, which they capture by ejecting barbed, poison-containing hypodermic threads from stinging cells.

The dragon fly nymphs are among the larger bottom predators: their hinged lower lips shoot out to capture other animals, then retrace to bring the victims to the actual chewing jaws. Flatworms crawl slowly across the bottom, feeding on animal carcases,while equally slow snails creep along, scraping algal coatings off dead sticks and other surfaces. Tube-dwelling rotifers, living in cases carefully constructed of rows of tiny pellets they have secreted, are attached to the same submerged sticks, but are left undisturbed by the snails. Small two-valved crustaceans swim close to the bottom, occasionally rising into the open water plankton populations overhead.

Most of the ponds contain small freshwater minnows, separated from their mainland relatives by inhospitable sand and salt bays. They may have arrived in the ponds as eggs carried on the legs or feathers of waterfowl. There seems to be little other explanation, since the island is a product of the sea itself and, even as a peninsula, has never shared freshwater streams with the continent.

The Thicket Zone A thicket zone of shrubs and small trees normally borders the interdune region on a barrier island (if you disregard the interruption caused by flats and freshwater ponds). As beach heath and grasses of the interdune give way to tangled stands of greenbrier and sawbrier, the going gets more difficult unless you are following a path. Wax myrtle is the dominant shrub, although its close relative, bayberry, is also very common, followed in lesser numbers by southern red oak, sheep sorrel, black cherry, and honeysuckle. Another abundant plant, almost as characteristic of the thicket area as wax myrtle, is poison ivy. In some localities, especially where salt marsh sloughs penetrate far into the island, poison ivy grows so vigorously it may develop into small trees not supported by any other plant.

The sandy soil grows darker and grayer in the thicket zone and supports a wide variety of low-lying plants. Red-topped British soldier lichens can be noticed at some distance despite their small size, and another lichen, old man's beard, similar to reindeer moss, grows on dead limbs of trees and shrubs. Other branching lichens sometimes occupy whole clearings in the thicket, crunching under your feet as you walk over them. Here and there you may come across the odd little earthstar, a puffball fungus adapted to dry conditions. On warm, dry days each grayish mottled sphere is wrapped around by dark triangular arms or "petals," but as soon as it rains the arms absorb water and unfold, exposing the puffball to the blows of pelting raindrops. Each drop compresses the puffball, which is nothing more than a sac containing millions of spores, so clouds of these microscopic spores are shot into the air to settle elsewhere. Under favorable conditions of humidity they germinate. An earthstar, as a true fungus, has to find nourishment from organic material such as decaying logs or mats of dead leaves.

A surprising discovery in the sandy thicket world is a fully developed mushroom erupting from under the sand, its sticky cap still covered by a layer of shining sand grains. The permanent underground part of the plant, consisting of weblike mycelial strands, is tapped into a supply of organic matter. There are several species of mushrooms living in the thicket zone and on the secondary dunes, and a couple of these appear to be dependent upon manure from ponies wandering through the region. Others with specific needs include a fleshy orange fungus that feeds upon dead bayberry branches lying on the sand.

As the thicket community grows more dense, and on into the pines, the sandy soil supports pricklypear cactus, whose yellow blooms beautify the area in the spring. Its purplish fruits mature in the late summer and the fall.

Next two pages: Dusty miller carpets sand so white it almost looks like snow. Adding to the illusion is the sparse spacing of the plants caused by sand's inability to hold life-supporting water. The effects created often suggest Oriental flower arrangements.

Preceding two pages: A Sika deer luxuriates in a meadow at the edge of pine woods. Sika are actually small Japanese elk imported and released here years ago by Boy Scouts. Cattle egrets flank the Sika.

The real secret to the greater abundance and diversity of plant life in the thicket zone is an increase in plant nutrients containing nitrogen, potassium, and phosphorus. As plants thrive, grow, die, and decay, their substance too gradually enriches the soil.

The thicket is home for many of Assateague's small vertebrates. It offers protection to cottontail rabbits, as well as field voles and other mice. Undoubtedly it makes good hunting ground for foxes and raccoons. A pale variation of Fowler's toad, the common toad of the eastern states, is everywhere. During the day the toads burrow beneath the sand or take refuge under protecting objects, but at night their calls are heard shrilling through the darkness; with a flashlight you will see their bulky shapes squatting on the sand. Hognose snakes and black racers thread their way through the thickets in search of these toads, mice, and other prey. The hognose snake is foolishly killed by some who mistake it for the copperhead, which it resembles. But there are no copperheads—or any other venomous snakes—on Assateague or Chincoteague Islands, and the hognose snake is beneficial. It has the habit of hissing and puffing to scare intruders off, but if this routine fails to discourage you, the hognose snake's next ploy is to play dead!

While amphibians and reptiles are present on Assateague in surprising numbers, their variety is not so great as on the mainland. Only certain ones have made their way by chance to the island, but once there they found an uncontested way of life and flourished. To have a reduced number of species of plants and animals is characteristic of islands everywhere, barrier or mid-oceanic. Of the more than 25 reptiles found on the nearby mainland, only half are present on the island. Assateague has but three species of amphibians, the mainland has 18. Amphibians, with their moist non-watertight skin, have difficulty with regulation of body fluids and a saltwater bay or salt marsh poses an insurmountable obstacle. Because of this there is no marine amphibian in the world.

Insects abound in the thicket zone: those that fly and those that live on plants or on the ground. Without pesticides to diminish their numbers and variety, a wide selection is available to students of insect life.

Like those in the interdune zone, some insects and ticks of the thickets can be distinctly unpleasant pests. During much of the year clouds of mosquitoes rise to follow every intruder. Because of the briers, it is difficult to escape with any speed the attentions of these determined mosquitoes and of the greenhead flies, whose bite draws blood.

The Tall Pines Toward the rear of the thicket area another transitional zone commences, perhaps with common elder and American holly. Then a few small conifers begin to appear, redcedar, scrub pine, or a few others. Looking just a bit farther you will see the island's largest trees, loblolly pines, looming over all else. This species tends to grow high anyway; but their elevation is aided by a secondary dune system that extends along much of the bayside of Assateague. These sand hills, in some places more than 12 meters (40 feet) high, are the result of centuries of blown sand being trapped by vegetation. It is always a relief and a pleasure to pass from the dense, often hot, thicket region with its snagging greenbriers and hordes of insects into cooler, open pine woods carpeted with pine needles on the rolling hills. Even on windy days the air is quiet here, although overhead, treetops toss and the wind whistles and sighs.

Tall pines provide a welcome change after the unrelieved openness of beach and dunes. They harbor familiar eastern woodland creatures such as the whitetail deer, and at least one endangered species, the Delmarva fox squirrel.

Actually the assemblage and variety of plants in the pine forest zone are much the same as in the thickets, but greenbrier, wax myrtle, poison ivy, holly, bayberry, and all the rest are not so thickly packed together. The high pines provide enough shade to be a limiting factor to the growth of shrubs; so the understory in loblolly woodlands is relatively open.

If you are quiet and patient, you may be rewarded by seeing the spotted, camouflaged Sika deer enter warily into the woodlands. Despite their increasing numbers on the island, these naturalized Asian-Americans remain shy of humans and blend so closely into the background they are difficult to make out even when close by. Only occasionally seen, gray, heavily scaled pine lizards dart along branches and up the rough bark of loblolly trunks. Birds also abound in the trees, not only many species of small perching birds, but also occasional hawks. The great horned owl, a major predator, is common throughout the year. The pine woods and adjoining thickets are excellent places for spotting warblers, sparrows, and numerous other small birds, especially during spring and fall migrations.

Loblolly pines do not achieve a true dominance over all other plants in the zone, as do live oak and other trees on barrier islands off North Carolina, but they are the largest and most populous of the trees on the secondary dunes of Assateague. In a few older areas the loblolly is all but absent and the most conspicuous trees are holly, wax myrtle, and redcedar. The loblolly does not easily propagate itself in regions where stands of trees are dense, because young pines need plenty of sunlight; hence, there is a scarcity of pine seedlings in the thick woods.

It is possible that at one time redcedar might have been the climax forest, for when winter storms erode the sea beach, large areas of old redcedar forest may be exposed with stumps and roots still intact.

Under the mat of pine needles carpeting the secondary dune, the soil, darker even than that of the thicket zone, consists of a sandy loam that is acidic and not very fertile. Ground-dwelling insects, spiders, and sowbugs (which are not bugs but terrestrial crustaceans) are plentiful on the forest floor, or beneath plant litter. Fowler's toad and a few species of snakes also enter the region, where hunting and shelter are as good as in the thickets.

Where tall pines overlook the bay or rise from small islets in it, an occasional osprey nest caps a dead tree or one with bare branches near the top. The nests appear to be massive, haphazard bundles of sticks, but in reality are well and securely made. Re-used year after year, they gradually increase in size. After a number of alarming years when the osprey population along the coast declined sharply because of weakened eggshells, the osprey is making a comeback. Now that DDT, the chief suspect in the problem, is much reduced in use, eggshell thickness is increasing and the developing embryos are not being crushed so frequently. Before long we may once again see osprey nests in the loblollies and on top of telephone and electric poles all along the coast.

American egrets and other herons find preferred roosts in the bayside pines from which they can look out over the quiet water. At times the dark green trees are draped in white, with egrets on almost every dead overhanging limb.

During severe storms, ponies and deer find refuge in the pine woodlands. Once Assateague was a heavily used grazing ground for domestic animals. Ponies, goats, cattle, sheep, and hogs were pastured there. None but the wild pony remains today. Overgrazing by large populations of herbivorous mammals must have had a serious effect upon the island in past centuries, probably denuding extensive areas of sand-holding vegetation. The small number of horses now remaining on the island appears to do little harm to its plants.

If you fly over the island, or are able to stand back from the pine woodland zone in open areas such as the flats, you should be able to see a gradual transition on both sides of the pines to other zones. The change from thicket to forest has already been described, but on the bay side loblollies usually give way to a narrow thicket zone, again consisting of elders, wax myrtle, and bayberry, perhaps right up to the margin of the high salt marsh. Where there is such a secondary thicket it is no more than a few meters wide. This thin belt of shrubs is buffeted by winds blowing across the open bay; so it may be affected by some salt spray, although waves in the bay seldom achieve great size. Scarring and reduced growth resulting from airborne salt is evident on many woody plants in this marginal thicket. It is also affected when storm tides occasionally rise in the bay and inundate the area if the terrain does not rise steeply enough toward the secondary dunes.

Visit the tall loblolly forest in all seasons if you can. In summer they soften the strong sea winds, their shade welcome relief from the searing heat of scrub thicket and interdune flats. In winter, the silence beneath these great towering trees makes you want to hold your breath. Snow drifts gently down through the powdered pine branches, settling in a thin, patched carpet upon the needles of the forest floor.

For some, the most pleasant season is spring, when foliage is out but the insects have not yet emerged in hordes; then you may walk under these lofty pines, examine the smaller plants of the forest floor, enjoy bird songs in the canopy above, and with luck catch occasional glimpses of deer and fox.

The forest is a reassuring place to be during a heavy storm: the tops of the tall supple pines toss about in the gale raging overhead but all is quiet where you stand, the air moving gently if at all. It is then that Sika and whitetail deer and ponies seek refuge as you have within the shelter and seclusion of the island's loblolly forest.

Sea Meadows

The last terrestrial zone of a barrier island consists of salt marsh, perhaps the most misunderstood of all coastal lands. People who pass by or travel through salt marshes find the flat terrain monotonous. They complain of the odor of decomposing cordgrass in the thick mud. If they must walk upon the marsh itself, they find the slippery, sticky sediment difficult to traverse. The footing is treacherous. Biting insects abound: vast numbers of breeding saltmarsh mosquitoes rise in clouds as thick as smoke. Many persons look upon salt marshes as wastelands—areas to be eliminated, or at best suitable only for a "muskrat economy."

In summer, it takes perseverance and courage to battle mud and mosquitoes and develop an appreciation for a coastal salt marsh. But the sight of a heron feeding along the banks of a slough, or hordes of posturing fiddler crabs rushing through the grassy salt meadows may compensate for any discomfort. Once you study and understand them and are appreciative of their complexities and values, salt marshes take on a beauty all their own. Even in winter when the dead, dry grass rattles in the breeze, there is a sere loveliness to the wide expanse of brown marshland.

The marsh complex may be approached from the bay or island by canoe or boat through a network of sloughs locally called guts. (Landing boats of any type on refuge lands is permitted only at designated sites.) A canoe is ideal for traversing salt marshes: it is quiet, easily handled, slender, and of shallow draft. But even a boat of shallow draft can become mired in the mud of shallow sloughs, especially if the tide is falling, so try to stay in the center of each channel. As you drift along making as little noise and disturbance as possible, the marsh world and its many inhabitants will open up to you.

It is fortunate that salt marshes are not readily accessible to multitudes of people for they are delicate habitats. The one thing least understood about marshes is their importance to the coastal—and world—ecosystem: a salt marsh is probably the earth's most productive natural cropland. A stand of cordgrass, the common grass of salt marshes, produces more nutrient material and stored energy than any other crop with the exception of cultivated sugar cane in the tropics. Much of this nutrient material is in the form of detritus, a rich nutrient "soup" made up of partially decomposed grasses and bacteria. The vital and often subtle role a salt marsh plays with regard to bays, estuaries, and the ocean itself goes unseen and unappreciated by most of us. Because we cannot easily enter a marsh, know little about its dynamics, associate it with swarms of mosquitoes, and think of it as odorous wasteland, we either neglect or purposely destroy the most valuable wetlands in existence.

How do salt marshes develop? They are visible reminders of the dynamics of a shallow coastal plain shoreline. With a slowly rising sea level over the centuries, it is inevitable that island overwash occur during storms. When it does, the huge surge of water carries enormous quantities of sand from offshore, from beaches and dunes. As the sheet of water loses velocity across the island and finally enters the bay, the sand it has transported drops out of suspension until a large, fan-shaped deposit accumulates on the far side of the island, extending out into the bay. It may, of course, cover a marsh that is already there; but whatever it invades, marsh, pine woods, or thicket, it continues out into the open shallow water of the bay, effectively widening the island. For a time, the bayside shore of Assateague where an overwash has occurred will consist of nothing more than a large fan of clean sand, barren of life.

Some erosion takes place along the newly deposited shore. Even if bay waves seldom achieve great size, the width of the bay, up to several kilometers, and its shallow depth provide an opportunity for steep waves to arise that possess a great deal of energy. There is enough shoreline erosion on the bay side of a barrier island to cut a marsh abruptly into sloughs with miniature cliff-edges, the sediments washing away to increase the turbidity of the bay where they eventually settle to enrich its bottom.

Soon marsh plants begin to appear at the margin of the new sand deposits and to work their way out toward deeper water. Some may simply rise through layers of sand covering their former bed; others extend runners from exposed marsh nearby. Also, seeds transported from marsh plants along the bay shore germinate where conditions are right and where competition from other plants is minimal. Once marsh plants are established, they trap sediment from the tides and add their own substance after seasonal decay in the quiet water. Gradually the sand fan turns dark with organic sediment, the bottom level rises, is exposed at high tide, and new land at last emerges: the island's progress has extended into the bay.

Marshes occur elsewhere, especially across the bay on the land side; but their origin and means of growth are different, for no overwash takes place there. On the continental shore, a rising sea (and bay) level gradually inundates the land, establishing the proper conditions for the growth of saltmarsh plants. In a few areas, although not at Assateague, salt marshes on both sides of the bay grow toward one another, joining except for a few deep tidal sloughs which allow twice-a-day flushing of this low-lying marine grassland.

Should overwash be prevented by, for example, the building of snow fences to encourage high primary dunes, a barrier island begins to wear away, eroded on both sides by wave and tidal action. Only if overwash is allowed can Assateague and similar barrier islands maintain themselves through natural processes. Barrier islands are flexible enough to give under the power of the ocean, but man's efforts are directed toward stabilizing beaches rather than allowing them to adjust to natural forces.

What's a Salt Marsh Good For? As already suggested, first impressions of a marsh are not always favorable. There is the strong odor of sulfur and of other compounds released from the mud; insects are ferocious in warm weather; the terrain lacks variation and supports only a few kinds of plants; the slippery and clinging mud, if walked upon, vibrates

Salt marsh vistas greet your approach to Assateague's south end. Their unruffled appearance little suggests the furious biotic activity that makes salt marshes 12 times as productive as forests. The secret lies with their specially adapted grasses.

Black-crowned night herons cry with a loud, barking kwok! *They occur worldwide, except in taiga and tundra belts and in Australia. Their young are so well camouflaged you usually see them only when they take flight.*

beneath your feet. Despite a general uniformity of plant populations, each marsh has its distinctive characteristics and in all seasons takes on an austere and fascinating beauty.

The plants so important to the permanency and productivity of a salt marsh are mostly grasses, primarily cordgrass. There are two species of cordgrass: first, the one typical of "high" marshes flooded only at high tide is *Spartina patens*. Often it is accompanied by spikegrass, *Distichlis*, as well. This is the area in which many birds nest during summer months and that land animals penetrate in search of food, for a wide variety of plants beside the dominant cordgrass may be found there. The common ones include water pennywort, bulrush, sea lavender, sedge, saltwort, and even an occasional seaside goldenrod. The cordgrass of high marshes used to be called saltmeadow hay, for at one time it was harvested extensively along the Atlantic coast. This was the grass that provided pasture for the domestic animals placed on Assateague Island long ago.

High-marsh cordgrass flourishes in a salty environment, whether as the result of tidal inundation or because of salt spray. It is able to withstand burial by sediment or erosion of surface sands and muds. No grass on the marsh or on the island is so tolerant of changing conditions. If, for instance, it is deeply buried by a sudden overwash, sooner or later, having grown up through the new sand deposits, it erupts above the surface, then spreads rapidly by sending out underground runners, or rhizomes. Because of this one grass, more than all the others combined, barrier islands grow in area and in extent, invading the bay through the consolidating of new sediments.

Toward the rear of the high-marsh zone on the island side the typical marsh plants mentioned above gradually give way to reeds and cattails, which are characteristic of more brackish, less salty, conditions. But where the high marsh slopes gently downward to be flooded regularly or even most of the time by the tides, "low" marsh conditions exist, with the second species of cordgrass, salt cordgrass (*Spartina alterniflora*), serving as the dominant plant. Low-marsh grass, because of its location, is not so subject to severe alterations of its habitat for it requires and receives frequent, periodic immersion. It is, however, even more productive of nutrients than

high-marsh cordgrass.

In a low marsh, mud remains saturated and is very difficult to traverse. Where sloughs cut through, their mud banks are abrupt, with chunks falling into the water to be carried back and forth by the tides. Here and there on marsh flats slight depressions may not flush well, allowing saltwater to remain behind with each tide. Because water evaporates in the sun at low tide, leaving salt behind, the salinity of these salt pans, or basins, is too extreme at first for plants to grow. Later, as sediment accumulates in a salt pan, it is invaded by pioneer plants and eventually reclaimed by the normal marsh vegetation. The small thick-stemmed saltwort is one of the first plants to appear around the margin of a salt pan, followed perhaps by a little seaside lavender. Dark coatings of blue-green algae cover the surface of the basin; these most primitive of plants are protected from drying by their sheaths of slimy mucus, which makes for a slippery footing.

Cordgrass is able to tolerate the normal salinities of bay water and of marsh mud because of special adaptations not present in other plants. Both cordgrass and spikegrass excrete superfluous salt by means of special cells along the edges and tips of the blades. If you go out early in the morning on a sunlit day, you are likely to see wide expanses of marsh glittering as though there had been a frost. Close examination reveals salt crystals along the edges of the blades, carried there through conducting vessels by water which has since evaporated. In this way a plant rids itself of excessive salt without causing damage to the living tissue, but enough salt remains in a blade of cordgrass to make it taste salty if you chew on it.

The cordgrass that accounts for such enormous production of organic matter in marshes is fed upon directly by only a few animals. One is the purple marsh crab, which cuts and eats short lengths of grass. But at least a quarter of the total marsh organic production is almost unavailable to most animals since it occurs on the surface of the mud as a result of photosynthetic activities by one-celled diatoms, flagellated cells, and filamentous green and blue-green algae.

When you look closely at patterns of marsh vegetation, you see tall, dense stands of cordgrass along the creeks where a natural levee is formed. Behind this fringe, cordgrass is shorter and not so dense. Where sand is deposited by overwash, or toward the back of a salt marsh where sand is creeping onto the mud from the island, there may be a distinct narrow band of saltwort rather than cordgrass or spikegrass.

Animals of a salt marsh are not of as wide a variety as elsewhere on the island or in the bay, but those present make up for it in numbers. Saltmarsh mosquitoes drive the adventuresome either to the haven of a parked car or tent or to the beach where strong sea breezes usually prevent the bloodthirsty insects from flying. During periods of summer drought, the same insects may not be especially bothersome, and ordinary insect repellents suffice.

There are more attractive inhabitants of salt marshes that are either transitory or permanent residents. Ponies graze in the high marsh. Herons of several kinds, willets, and rails may be seen in the cordgrass or perched on nearby loblolly pines; but most of them move on with the seasons. Other animals live the year around on, or in, the peaty mud and in the grass itself. Examination of cordgrass should reveal numerous small saltmarsh snails climbing up and down the blades. Below, on the surface of the mud, other snails, whitish periwinkles, browse on detritus and algae. Farther out, where the marsh begins to disappear and true mud flats take over, the dark, battered-looking mud snails congregate in great numbers. Toward the creek banks are clusters of heavy-ribbed mussels with attaching threads holding them securely to rootstocks when the tides begin to tug at them. Ribbed mussels are filter feeders and derive all their nourishment from the heavily laden tidal water washing over them twice a day.

When the tide is out, you may be startled by a loud rushing noise in the tall grass; it sounds like a local wind, yet the grass blades remain still. If you are quiet, you will be treated to the sight of a swarm of fiddler crabs on the move to feeding grounds. Normally they stay fairly close to their burrows where they find security under a plug of mud during high tide. When the water level drops, they emerge to forage in the mud for organic debris. Female fiddlers eat busily with their two small claws; but the males must acquire all their nourishment with only one, for the other claw is grossly enlarged as a display appendage, with which they threaten other males in defense of their territory or which they wave up and down to attract females. This one claw of the male, despite its great size, does slight damage, for only the tips meet and the two concave fingers are incapable of crushing or shearing. Usually there are two species of fiddler crab living in the same general region, although their habits and precise zones of preference differ somewhat. One, the large, red-jointed fiddler crab, is distinctly in the minority and somewhat solitary. The other, a smaller one, which has a bluish spot between the eyes on its hard carapace, a spot that changes color with the rhythm of the tides, is the crab that occurs in huge numbers.

The purple marsh crab mentioned earlier is not so frequently seen. It is a stout, heavily clawed animal that builds a burrow with a mud hut and "porch" over the opening. It does not feed on organic detritus in the mud as fiddlers do, but prefers to cut down and harvest cordgrass. All these, fiddlers and purple marsh crabs, are in fact only semiterrestrial, because their life cycles embrace saltwater stages. Females release their eggs on a flood tide: the eggs then hatch into tiny spined creatures that swim as members of the plankton. They go through several developmental stages, each quite different from the other, until finally, if able to survive this long, they emerge onto the mud to take up residence as land dwellers. Even then each crab must keep its gill chambers moist to allow for respiration.

Lesser creatures abound on the muddy surface of the marsh and its pools, and in the upper ends of sloughs. There are small amphipod crustaceans, some small, almost transparent shrimp, and a number of near-microscopic simpler crustaceans that burrow into the soft, flocculent bottom debris. Some of these small animals wash back and forth with each tide, but others are capable of remaining more or less in one area. There are different species of mud-dwelling worms, some of them colorful ribbon worms that fragment themselves when picked up. The population of microscopic life forms is beyond reckoning, whether you consider roundworms, protozoans, or bacteria that are so important to the decay and disintegration of the rich vegetation when it dies and falls to the marsh surface.

Greater numbers and varieties of plants and animals live in the creeks and sloughs: they are more related to the bay's inhabitants than are those of the marsh. The confines of the sloughs afford them just the right kind of environment in which to live, both for protection and for food. It is also a suitable nursery ground for their young or larval stage.

The important thing to remember about salt marshes is that in their plant-production activities they lock up enormous amounts of chemical energy into living form. Animals make use of this energy either directly or indirectly, according to their food habits. When the plants decay, the simpler molecular compounds into which they disintegrate form nutrients for other plants, especially microscopic diatoms that are a sort of floating "grass" present in all coastal marine waters. (The term "grass" does not imply filaments or long blades, but reflects the abundance of the diatoms and their function as the pastures of the sea.) The diatoms are eaten by small animals, which soon become food for larger creatures. In addition, some of the nutrients are returned by tides to the salt marshes, where they nourish cordgrass and other plants that are flooded periodically. The cycling of chemical nutrients is brought about initially by the action of the bacteria of decay that are so abundant in marsh muds and are primarily responsible for the odors given off by marshes. While cordgrass makes use of some of the nutrient chemicals released by such decay, the greater percentage of it is flushed out by the tides to nourish bay-dwelling and eventually oceanic organisms. Thus a salt marsh is a major and vital part of the marine ecosystem, one that needs to be preserved and understood more fully.

The great productivity of a salt marsh is maintained by the constant daily tidal flooding and by periodic overwash of the island. Nutrients are brought in and flushed out again, constantly being reworked and reduced in size until they are only molecular. Since a salt marsh is more than 12 times as productive as a forest, the nutrients it produces are obviously of inestimable importance not only to the bay behind a barrier island, but also to the entire coastal environment. Some biologists feel that the salt marshes, along with coastal plankton, largely nourish the entire oceans. That is a great ecological responsibility, but many people continue to find these lands undesirable because of their odors, muds, and insects and want to drain or fill them. The destruction of a salt marsh may not have an immediate, observable effect upon the population of the seas; but ultimately the effect will be felt.

The Bay, A Sea in Miniature Where the marsh meets the bay we once again face the dilemma of attempting to decide where the marine environment begins and the land ends. There is no precise answer; with sea-level changes occurring through geological time, and tides causing daily fluctuations, one of these two habitats overrides the other and is itself later overridden. Passing through the marshes of Assateague, you soon encounter small waterways that begin in modest fashion but grow into the larger creeks or sloughs devoid of surface vegetation and with a character all their own. Many are deep, and often the swiftness of the tide-driven current is evident when you see floating objects race by as you stand on the muddy shore. The ebb tide is usually dark and opaque, evidence of the enormous quantities of organic detritus being removed from the draining salt marsh.

If you could look beneath the surface of a slough and see the animals it contains clearly, their variety would come as a surprise. The most abundant fishes are small ones: killifish, anchovies, and a host of young marine fishes; later, after these fish achieve greater size, they live beyond the bay out in the sea. Sloughs and the protected bay are vast nursery areas for many fishes and other animals that, while they still are small and vulnerable, cannot withstand the rigors of offshore sea life.

The Chincoteague and Sinepuxent Bays are shallow on the island side, principally because of the deposition of overwash sediments, but they are much deeper on the mainland side where the bay waters are slowly but persistently riding up over the continent. The result is that waters on the island side are more easily warmed by the sun and the shallow, sedimentary bottom is richer with organic muds. In short, bays are better nursery regions and better habitat for those lesser invertebrates needing such conditions for survival.

When a slough is fairly clear, a rare event in summer because of heavy algae growth, you can see the bottom and find evidence of a few of the lives it supports. First, swimming crabs such as the blue crab and lady crab may be seen resting quietly or swimming with paddlelike rear legs. Smaller mud crabs, colored like the slough bottom, live in large numbers among hard, sheltering objects where they can be found crawling about as they feed. There are several species of these small mud crabs, but with their dull coloration and heavy, black-tipped claws they are difficult for the casual observer to tell apart. In places where low-marsh cordgrass reaches far out into the bay, mud snails abound. Their shells are not handsome, but blackish and battered looking, often with the tip of the spiral shell worn off. In numbers defying imagination, they at times carpet the bottom as they eat organic detritus and mud-dwelling algae, mostly diatoms that cover the soft sediments.

Attempting to see the bottom out in the bay is another matter. At times one of the swimming crabs will come close to the surface before descending again, but you will not see any of the mud crabs or the large, sluggish spider crabs. Sting rays and skates lie almost motionless on the bottom, only the gentle fluttering of their gill openings, or spiracles, giving an indication of their presence. If you disturb one inadvertently, however, it will explode from the muddy sand and rush off, flying through the water with gracefully waving winglike fins before settling once again on the bottom. Then, with a ripple of these same fins, it scoops sand over its body, hiding itself from view.

At times the bay may contain a number of jellyfish, a few species of which you would do best to avoid. There may be enormous populations of small, nonstinging creatures known as comb jellies. Not true jellyfish at all, they swim by beating eight rows of ciliary comb plates, rather than by jet propulsion. On sunny days, the rapidly moving comb plates may catch the light and, acting as prisms, cause waves of iridescent color to flow down their transparent bodies. Comb jellies feed upon plankton and are entirely harmless to people. Also there are true jellyfish that either do not sting or have stings so feeble they can hardly be felt. Some, no larger than the head of a pin, are the alternate generation to the many kinds of stalked hydroids that live attached to submerged rocks and on wharf pilings. The reddish sun jelly and

Next two pages: "Cursed beauty" might characterize jellyfish, whose bodies are more than 95 percent water. Not all sting, but avoid those you don't know! The notorious Chesapeake sea nettle, a real stinger, is common here. Shown are its juvenile and adult stages, respectively.

white or colorless moon jelly are examples of larger harmless forms, the sun jelly capable of producing only the mildest sting and the moon jelly none at all. But the bay may also harbor the notorious Chesapeake sea nettle, a fairly large jellyfish distributed along the entire Atlantic coast. You will have to learn to distinguish it from the harmless species, for its color may range from rose through yellow to white. It has a heavy growth of tentacles around the outside of its umbrella-shaped bell, while the others have most of their tentacles grouped more toward the center. A sea nettle's sting is one to avoid; it burns like fire.

Across the island, on the sea beaches, an occasional Portuguese-man-o'-war may be cast up or seen floating just offshore. These animals are not true jellyfishes at all but colonies of stinging polyps closely related to the bunches of harmless hydroids that grow plantlike on submerged solid objects up and down the coast and in bays and inlets. A Portuguese-man-o'-war should not be approached in the water, for it trails its tentacle-like polyps several meters from the floating blue and pink balloon at the surface. Even on the wet sand of the beach, a detached tentacle cast up by the waves can deliver a severe sting to a careless barefoot passerby.

A hydromedusa's near-transparency reveals its inner structure. Jellyfish snare and paralyze passing organisms with trailing tentacles. The tentacles then contract and draw this food to the mouth.

Back in the bay bottom, distinct craters, mounds, and castings betray the presence of worms and bivalve molluscs living beneath the sandy mud. With experience, each feature is recognizable as the home of a distinct species of invertebrate; but its inhabitant may be difficult to obtain. Often the burrows are long and curved, with more than one entrance; and any activity, such as digging, releases clouds of sediment into the water, completely obscuring the area and allowing the animal residents to escape the collector. At the proper season for an individual species, egg masses may be found emerging from a burrow or lying on the muddy bottom. One common egg mass is the shape and size of a large sausage but nearly transparent except for adhering mud particles. It is produced by a truly formidable invertebrate, the lugworm, which grows to the diameter of a man's thumb and a length of more than 15 centimeters (6 inches). The lugworm makes its home in a U-shaped tube well down in the mud and does not emerge into view.

Plants of the Sea True seaweeds grow in the bay where water does not move forcefully in and out of sloughs, or in shallow water just off the salt marshes. Thin, flat, crumpled fronds of emerald-green sea lettuce and delicately branched red seaweeds are the most common. They live abundantly on the island side where shallow water allows sunlight to penetrate the usually turbid water. Some algae grow profusely enough to serve as binding agents in the mud and, like cordgrass, are sediment traps for particles suspended in the weak currents out in the bay. If you search such an area, large numbers of small shrimp, usually the common glass shrimp, dart forth in alarm. Captured in a bottle, they appear almost transparent except for their digestive system, eyes, and few splotched color cells. Some of the females undoubtedly will be carrying egg masses under their abdomens during the summer months.

Algae of the bay are more varied than you might think. Green algae other than sea lettuce flourish in the warm illuminated water: long strands or filaments, branched or unbranched, tubular and flattened, each a distinct species. Brown algae similar to those found on rocky marine shorelines farther north are present in Chincoteague Bay, as are other longer, ropey forms with air bladders distributed along their length or toward the ends of fronds. Despite their classifying name, red algae can be pink, purple, black, or even greenish, and they also can be bushy or delicately branched. Blue-green algae, the most primitive of all, sometimes coat marsh muds with a blackish, slippery layer. All provide both food and shelter for the smaller animals of the bay.

Circulation of water within the bay is rather weak, the water being driven mostly by wind and lessened tidal currents. Nevertheless, it is sufficient to allow a constant exchange of nutrients and dissolved gases necessary for plants and animals—both those that live on the bottom or swim freely and those that burrow deep beneath the loose sediments.

A bay behind a barrier island is essentially trapped sea water, in contact with the ocean only through an occasional inlet passing through the island. Because these inlets are narrow and do not allow massive exchange of water, the tides in a bay are relatively slight: about a meter at the inlets, but only 13 centimeters (5 inches) or so in the bay behind Assa-

Next three pages: The geometry of life appears in the bay's secret holdings. The greatly magnified microscopic opossum shrimp's elongation contrasts with the radial structures of scallop and peacock worm shown on the third page.

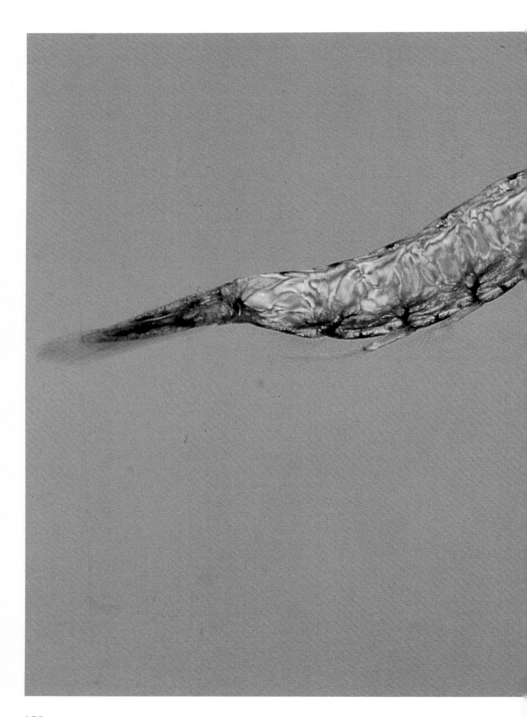

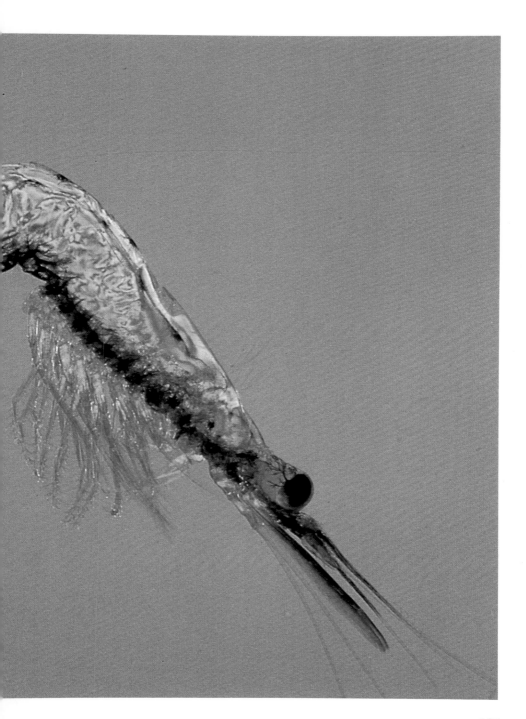

Amphithoe longimana

Scallop

Skate embryo in "mermaid's purse"

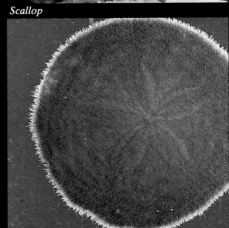

Echinarachinius parma

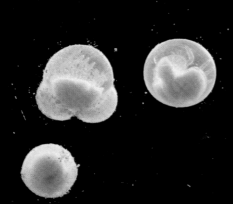

Limulus eggs

Peacock worm

teague Island. Since currents are gentle, sediment builds up until the entire bay becomes a shallow body of water, more so on the island side than on the mainland shore. Salinities in the bay can be either lower than sea water, because of the runoff of inland rains, or greater, if there is little rain but a great deal of evaporation from the bay surface. Organisms living there must be able to cope with these irregularly varying conditions.

An inlet is usually more heavily populated and productive than inner regions of the bay. Temperature and dissolved oxygen levels are more constant, with deeper water harboring a large number of animals that come in or out, either with the tides or of their own accord, to feed and reproduce. Strong currents in inlets scour the bottom, keeping it deep and clean, with coarse sand and shell rubble covering the substrate. True marine creatures not always found in the bay can live here without difficulty. Sea stars seeking molluscan food, sand dollars under the rubble, sea urchins wedged in depressions, jet-propelled scallops, and stout rock crabs are but a few. Inlets are good places for fishing because so many finfish find it profitable to wait there for food as it is swept in by the swift tidal currents.

Even though Chincoteague Bay is not a terrestrial environment, it is as much related to the barrier island of Assateague as are the other zones already discussed. Up to 8 kilometers (5 miles) wide and more than 300 square kilometers (115 square miles) in area, it is far larger than all these put together. It averages only a little more than a meter in depth, but some areas are twice that and others less. Despite its shallowness, its huge water volume provides an extensive habitat for marine organisms. Area for area, it is far more productive than the loose, sandy soils of the island. Both habitats, island and bay, can claim the salt marshes, which periodically are either exposed or submerged.

Marine Pastures If you fly over the bay or travel across its surface, you notice dark patches on the bottom which indicate a special kind of submerged vegetation. It consists of two species of seed plants that have "gone to sea" and are in no way related to the algae. One of these, widgeongrass, or *Ruppia*, is characteristic of quiet waters without major currents. (It is not a true grass but a pondweed.) It prefers rather dense muddy bottoms and is sensitive to reduced levels of illumination when the water grows turbid, and to extremes in temperature. Its many small and tender leaves are eaten extensively by a wide variety of waterfowl, including two dozen species of ducks, two kinds of geese, and swans.

The other pondweed "grass," eelgrass, or *Zostera* is somewhat better known and more widely distributed along the Atlantic coast. It withstands vigorous currents and prefers open, deeper water with less muddy bottoms, even pure sand. Because these conditions are not prevalent in the bay behind Assateague, eelgrass is not so widespread as widgeongrass. In Chincoteague Bay, despite a reduced transparency, *Zostera* grows in shallow water, where its long, tapelike leaves can be seen waving in the clearer areas. Because it has a wide tolerance to changes in salinity, it does well near inlets where the water may be deep and quite transparent. The leaves, seeds, and roots of eelgrass are eaten by more than two dozen waterfowl species, particularly those that dabble about for food or dive beneath the surface. It forms the main diet of the brant, which is populous in the bay, and of large flocks of Canada geese that elect to remain there for long periods.

Eelgrass beds establish conditions that encourage the presence and growth of many marine organisms, scallops for example. These remarkable bivalve molluscs, with their two rows of sapphire-blue eyes, swim by jet propulsion. They flourish as members of the eelgrass community. When the eelgrass was infected by a microscopic organism several decades ago and largely died out up and down the coast, scallops, as well as brant, and other creatures depending upon *Zostera* in one way or another were seriously reduced in numbers. But eelgrass has made a good though slow recovery, and other organisms in the community are also increasing to their former numbers.

Studies of the *Zostera* community can be rewarding and instructive, because of the many different forms of life that live in close association on any available surface. Unlike algae, whose slippery, mucus-coated fronds discourage the attachment of other organisms, eelgrass leaves provide a suitable place for settlement by a host of lesser plants and small animals. Diatoms, encrusting algae, some pink and coralline in nature, give the long leaves a splotched and fuzzy appearance. In addition, attaching animals such as hydroids, bryozoans, and colonial sea squirts, can be found on the long, gracefully swaying blades. Among the miniature forests provided by attached microplants on each blade are hordes of tiny crustaceans, protozoans, worms, snails, sea spiders, and other bizarre creatures. They cannot live successfully on the bay bottom because of the thick suffocating sediment, and there are few solid uncluttered places on which to grow along the shoreline of the bay; so the long, firm leaves of eelgrass become attractive surfaces on which to grow and feed. Competition for space in the bay is keen.

As you look along one blade of eelgrass you will see that down at its base there are few attaching life forms. As you follow up the tape-like leaf, pioneers begin to appear. Farther on, more crowd in until finally, toward the end of the leaf, which is the oldest part, attaching organisms are so thick that the green leaf cells beneath are denied sufficient sunlight and are dying, turning dark and allowing the leaf to become tattered and frayed.

Studies of the animals living on eelgrass have revealed a complex series of interrelationships between dominant and more submissive species, also between those that do well under conditions of higher water velocity as opposed to those that favor quieter water. Some prey upon others, but most graze upon the near-microscopic plant life growing on eelgrass blades, or upon accumulated organic debris. Many exhibit distinct seasonal fluctuations, so communities present at one time of year may show quite different associations of life at other seasons.

Certainly the grassy areas, whether of eelgrass or widgeongrass, support the greatest amount of life in the bay. Crustaceans such as blue crabs and ghost shrimps are prevalent, as are killifish, silversides, anchovies, young menhaden and other finfishes. Beneath the grass and in more open spaces, a completely different association exists: animals that dwell beneath the bottom. Generally the dominant organism in this community is the hard clam, an effective filter feeder, which strains quantities of organic matter from the turbid water. Hard clams do well in sandy rather than muddy substrates, a

People compete with horseshoe crabs, rays, and other natural predators to harvest tasty clams from Assateague's marine pastures. You can gather clams without a license at low tide along Toms Cove. The only equipment you need is a bucket, boots, and a digging implement. At high tide and throughout most of the bay behind Assateague, wading with a long-handled rake is necessary. Commercial watermen use tongs and work from a boat (above right). Clams are filter feeders. They strain organic matter from the turbid waters, settling out in beds on sandy or muddy bottoms. Several sizes of the quahog (hardshelled) clam are found. They are called cherrystones, steamers, or little necks when small and chowders when large. To promote richer commercial harvests of this important species, seed clams (right) are sown in the water.

preference also shared by the less abundant softshell clam, or steamer, and the razor clam.

When these clams are young and not too deeply embedded they are prey for the horseshoe crab. This is not actually a crab or even a crustacean. It is a living relict of ages past, the only one of its kind, distantly related to the spiders. It is not poisonous or harmful to man. As it moves its great shield-shaped body lightly over the bottom, either by walking or by swimming with fanning gills, it will occasionally settle into the soft bottom and grope about for food. A clam picked up by its weakly clawed legs is then crushed in a grinding mill formed by its "shoulders," for it has no true jaws. The soft parts of the clam's body are then sucked into the horseshoe crab's extensive digestive system. Because horseshoe crabs molt their exoskeleton to grow, it is not uncommon to find a complete, neatly shed external skeleton along the shore. How do you tell the difference between one of these and a dead horseshoe crab? If it is a cast-off skin, it will be completely empty and separated, or "unzipped," along the front margin. If it is simply a dead animal, you will certainly know it! Horseshoe crabs caught on the beaches in the spring when they come up to lay eggs, may be flipped over by gulls and eviscerated.

A horseshoe crab demonstrates one good example of an important biological principle: commensalism. On the ventral gills, which are arranged like the leaves of a book, you may find little white flatworms of the genus *Bdelloura*. They are not parasites, as often thought, and are not totally restricted to the horseshoe crab, though that is where they most commonly occur. It's a good place to live, but not essential to the flatworm, and the horseshoe crab is not affected for good or ill.

In an overall sense, the importance of bays behind barrier islands lies in their being nursery areas for hordes of marine creatures that otherwise could not survive the rigors of the open sea. For this reason alone it is important that barrier-island bays be kept open and unpolluted, and that boat traffic and dredging activities be kept to a minimum.

Inhabitants of the bay read like a who's who of familiar marine animals. Even an occasional open-sea creature from far away gets carried through the tidal inlets to show up unexpectedly in the bay. Good places for collecting or observing exist along stone jetties and on wharf pilings. Old, beached fishing boats may support a large assemblage of marine organisms on their rotting hulks. The most apparent life forms are those that are firmly attached to submerged surfaces. They include red, green, and brown seaweeds and a host of animals: sponges, hydroids, sea anemones, striped flatworms, tube-dwelling segmented worms, barnacles, mussels, sea squirts, and bryozoans or moss animals. In addition, there are motile animals that browse either upon organic detritus or upon algae, and the predators that actively hunt other marine animals. The hunters include free-swimming segmented worms, sea stars, sea slugs, predatory snails, sea spiders, and many kinds of crustaceans such as crabs, scuds, skeleton shrimp, mantis shrimp, and sea roaches.

Next two pages: Great blue herons often still-hunt fish in sight of wildlife refuge roads. When startled they emit a loud and raucous grak or Kraak, seeming to emphasize their 122-centimeter (48-inch) length. They fly with the neck folded back on the shoulder, which distinguishes them in flight from cranes near their size.

Chincoteague National Wildlife Refuge

At the southern end of Assateague Island, opposite the town of Chincoteague on the bay island of the same name, a large tract of land and water has been set aside as a national wildlife refuge. Here native plants and animals are protected and managed by the Fish and Wildlife Service.

The refuge serves wildlife in many ways, providing resting and feeding places, and at times nesting sites, for migratory waterfowl, game birds, and songbirds, as well as for other indigenous animals. Management programs have modified the area to support and enhance wildlife and ways have been devised for people to enjoy viewing birds and mammals and to reach formerly inaccessible habitats or to engage in wildlife-related recreational pursuits.

The most obvious change has been the impounding of former inlets and small bays or coves, creating large water-conservation pools. A number of these are purely fresh, supplied only by rainwater and the water table underlying the island. Into others saline water is periodically pumped from Toms Cove, to maintain water levels and to encourage certain plant growth. Aquatic vegetation differs in fresh-, salt-, and brackish-water impoundments, so that a variety of food plants is available for waterfowl that have

distinct preferences. When saltwater is pumped in, planktonic life forms, including larval crabs and other marine creatures, are carried along. Some survive and flourish, perhaps growing rapidly and to great size. For others the warm, quiet, uncirculating waters of a large pond are too different from their marine environment and they are unable to make the necessary adjustment.

These more than half-dozen, large impoundments all differ from one another. Each year they support a greater variety of waterfowl and shore birds that spend winters or the entire year here. Some nest and raise their young along the banks; others fly on to the northern latitudes to do so.

For birders the attraction of the refuge is enormous. Depending on the season of the year and the habitat, you may see the sparkling white of greater snow geese and tundra and mute swans, several species of dabbling ducks, glossy ibis probing the shallows, or a solitary black-crowned night heron standing motionless by the shore. You will watch sanderlings pattering along the narrow, sandy shoreline. You may thrill at the sight of dozens of great egrets standing out in bold white relief against the tall loblolly pines in which they roost. Among them, equally brilliant, may be a little blue heron in its white phase, the wind ruffling its plumed feathers. Gliding far above is a solitary osprey. This great fish hawk has made a comeback after a protracted bout with DDT brought it close to extinction along the Atlantic shore. Through a small slough or gut a large black snake swims with its head raised above its sinuous body; and the brown, rounded head of an industrious muskrat cleaves a V-shaped wake as it swims earnestly toward its burrow in the bank.

Algae choke many of the ponds; they are the fine filaments of freshwater species, floating at the surface because of gas bubbles trapped beneath their interwoven meshes. In spring some of the wide algal mats are colored yellow by the clouds of pine pollen that are blown from the thick stands of loblolly along the island shores.

Once there were few, if any, wood ducks on the island. They were common inland and along the Pocomoke River, but Assateague Island offered few attractive habitats in which they could nest. Biologists at the national wildlife refuge placed nesting

"Wall-to-wall Canada geese" (top) might describe the Delmarva peninsula in fall, much to the hunter's delight. We appear to spy on the feeding of this snow egret photographed through tall grasses. Graceful tundra swans (bottom) are a portrait painter's dream. Perhaps no bird here seems more a part of the water itself. These swans breed in the Arctic, where they nest on small islets in tundra lakes and marshes.

boxes on posts in some of the shallow ponds, and brought in a number of wood ducks from a breeding station. Soon some boxes were occupied by these most colorful of American waterfowl. Today some wood ducks have found suitable places to nest in the tall pines; the females that had originally been established in the refuge returned voluntarily. Because they are the dominant sex, females lead new males into the region, and broods are now being raised successfully and naturally on Assateague Island.

Bobwhite, today heard everywhere throughout the pines, were released some years ago near the refuge headquarters building. They are equally abundant at the northern end, where they were introduced by property owners before the national seashore was established. Their distinctive calls are heard throughout the island.

The handsome spotted Sika deer, introduced to the United States from Asia many years ago, now inhabits Assateague Island. It outnumbers the native whitetail deer in the refuge portion of the island. There seems to be little competition for food or space; both species intermingle freely, though they do not interbreed. Both graze upon similar vegetation during much of the year, but in winter Sika depend largely upon greenbrier, in which they also bed down, while whitetails eat bark from trees and rest in poison-ivy thickets. Today it is possible for you to see both species of deer here with some frequency, especially if you wait near their distinctive forest trails.

Some parts of the refuge have been enhanced for wildlife by regulated burning, which does not damage larger trees. This management technique returns nutrients to the soil and replaces the natural understory with plant growth providing better wildlife forage. In such burned areas the more open understory better enables you to see deer and other wild inhabitants.

Refuges, managed by the U.S. Fish and Wildlife Service, are concerned primarily with animals and their habitats and stress programs that benefit wildlife yet allow public use. Uses that promote appreciation and understanding of wildlife are encouraged. National seashores, areas of the National Park System, are recreation oriented and encourage activities compatible with the preservation of native plants and animals. On a refuge, a predatory species such as fox or raccoon might be regulated to protect nesting waterfowl; in a national park, only a non-native species would be controlled. Yet many national park areas, including Assateague, allow recreational fishing. In Assateague and some other National Park System recreation areas, hunting is also permitted, under state regulations.

So far, there has been no need to transplant freshwater fish into the refuge's impoundments for fish-eating ducks and herons. Already established, apparently by natural means, in the ponds are mullet, white perch, eel, gizzard shad, some of the sunfishes such as bluegills, and the curious little nest-building sticklebacks. Probably there are other fishes present as well and undoubtedly more will appear over the years. How? Perhaps through intentional planting, but maybe by their gelatinous eggs that can stick to the feet and feathers of aquatic birds. In the saline ponds a few marine or estuarine fishes may be able to survive after being pumped in as tiny fry.

What effect has refuge management had upon animal populations? Examples abound. Refuges along the Atlantic Coast are now heavily relied upon by the gadwall, which like the black duck is presently a year-round resident, breeding and wintering on Assateague, where it never did before. More blue-winged teal and mallards nest on the island than formerly; pintails, while they don't nest in the refuge, spend winters in this protected area.

The Chincoteague National Wildlife Refuge is a haven for certain endangered and threatened species or those that may be placed on such lists. These include the Delmarva Peninsula fox squirrel, peregrine falcon, and piping plover. Other species distinctly unusual in this area of the coast appear from time to time. In the early 1980s the brown pelican began arriving in spring migrations and now it nests on isolated islands in nearby Chincoteague Bay. As years pass, more wildlife species may be expected to appear and find favorable habitat in the island refuge.

Next two pages: The ponies' calm grazing and their open, almost pastoral habitat make it hard to consider them the wild animals they are. Assateague ponies do not exhibit great activity; they walk quietly and purposefully from one grazing area to the next. Freshwater ponds are plentiful throughout the island.

Ponies—Wild and Free

For all its wealth of native plants and animals, the island's best known inhabitants, the wild ponies, are almost certainly immigrants to this barrier strip of beach. Although the distant ancestors of all horses originated in North America, today's are descended from Old World horses. Legend has it that Assateague's ponies arrived with pirates or from the wreck of a Spanish galleon. Most likely any horses shipwrecked here bred subsequently with horses pastured on the island by colonists during the mid-17th century. The colonists may possibly have practiced such grazing to escape taxation (see pages 14-16), because the island pasture-land was free. Natural selection had its effects in this rigorous habitat, and today the ponies are small, sturdy, shaggy animals.

About one-half of Assateague's ponies live on the northern (Maryland) end of the island. Kept between 120 and 150 head, and composed of many distinct subgroups or bands, they are managed by the National Park Service. The Virginia herd, also living in a number of subgroups, are owned by the Chincoteague Volunteer Fire Company and occupy the southern (Virginia) portion of Assateague Island and adjacent islands of Chincoteague National Wildlife Refuge. A fence at the state line separates the herds, and it is the Virginia ponies that are rounded up by the firemen on the last Wednesday of each July for the famous swim and auction.

The ponies' foaling season generally runs from April to September with perhaps half the ponies being born in May. Overall the sex ratio of the foals is one to one but this fluctuates widely from year to year. In a given year nearly all ponies born may be of one sex. The average pony will live to be at least 15 years old. A 20-year-old pony would be considered old. There are natural checks on their lifespan, mainly disease, internal parasites, and malnutrition. The malnutrition is related to aging because it involves the wearing down of their teeth. Half their diet is saltmarsh cordgrass, which is abrasive and salty, contributing to teeth wear.

The ponies are reasonably familiar with people

and are not overly shy—some enter campgrounds to beg for food—but they are wild animals not disciplined to the whims and commands of humans. Each year a number of people are seriously injured by bites and kicks. Perhaps the most rewarding thing you can do is to study them from a medium distance, perhaps with field glasses, observing their behavior when they are unaffected by your presence. It is surprising what a few hours of watching will reveal.

The ponies spend their lives on the island, summer and winter. Those in the southern end have more extensive ranges for grazing than those to the north and may be easier for the casual visitor to find and watch since they are more numerous. But the northern part of the island is more open, and most of the following observations were made there.

Except for thickets and the loblolly pine forests, there is no shelter, and the hardy little ponies withstand the harshest weather openly. But often at night, and always when great storms arrive, they seek protection in the deepest part of the forest and shrubbery. In winter they spend much of the time grazing on dead marsh grasses. They tend to rest more and graze less in summer, especially during the heat of midday; at night they may graze on saltmarsh cordgrass for hours on end. While they frequent the dunes to feed on beach grass, salt marshes are the most attractive grazing areas to Assateague ponies, and it is here more than anywhere else that they may not be alone during their feeding. Often they are accompanied by cattle egrets and starlings, either of which may be seen feeding alongside on the ground or perched on the ponies' backs. An observer at the southern end of the island has seen an egret remain on a pony for up to an hour at a time. Cattle egrets, originally from Africa, not only find insect food in ground disturbed by ponies, but they also pick insect and tick parasites off their hides.

Adult ponies rest while standing. You may not often see an adult pony lying on the ground, but when you do, it will be down either with its legs doubled up underneath and head upright, or on its side with legs outstretched and head on the ground. In either case, a pony can jump up quickly and be on the move at once if alarmed. Foals, preferring not to rest standing up, frequently lie down, a form of behavior common to most young mammals.

Each of the main herds has subgroups, each being a rather loosely organized assembly of mares, yearlings, foals, and often one stallion. Such a subgroup is not constant, but may change in its composition. Ponies have definite home ranges, but these are very broad and they move about within them, often guided more or less by the group stallion.

As with all horses, there is a great deal of interaction between individuals. Grooming, for example, may be solitary or mutual between two animals, upon invitation. Grooming, instinctive in a pony, is often a matter of comfort, necessity, and perhaps reassurance. Self-grooming consists of twitching local muscles to discourage flies, shaking the head or the whole body to get rid of bothersome insects, rolling in the sand, scratching or hitting the body with a hind leg, stamping, tail swishing, nibbling, rubbing against trees (or electric poles in mid-island) and so on. At the Virginia end of the island, there are favorite rubbing trees with limbs smoothed from long use and covered with pony hairs caught in splinters. At times, ponies may seem to be waiting in line to use such a grooming post.

Mutual grooming includes most of the same activities, but one animal, usually the younger or subservient pony, approaches the other with a definite invitation consisting of a particular expression: mouth partly open to expose the lower teeth, and ears cocked forward. The second pony may elect to accept the invitation, or to refuse by laying back its ears and even threatening to bite. Occasionally one will really bite or even rear up and deliver a powerful kick, which usually fails to land. If an invitation is accepted, then both ponies, facing each other, nibble at head, mane, and neck. When the greenhead flies are especially bad, as they are in midsummer, the ponies may gallop away from areas of heavy infestation, or end up side by side, head to tail, each swishing away the insects from the other's head for hours on end. Ticks and female mosquitoes also attack the ponies; but only greenhead flies are clearly bothersome, their painful bites at times so irritating that the ponies wade out into the ocean surf or into the bay, where they may stand quietly for hours.

During daytime the groups of a given herd are rather widely dispersed unless something has disturbed them; they gather more closely only as darkness falls or in northeasters and winter storms. They can be watched easily in daytime, but of course see you and one another clearly too. What one pony does is often of interest to the others and may be imitated. If one rolls in the sand in the interdunes, another may soon follow suit. If all are resting and one rises or strolls off to graze or to seek water, others are likely to do the same. When they rest, either standing or lying, they do so close to one another.

But all is not entirely peaceful within groups or herds. An individual for some reason may be ostracized and excluded from a herd. Ill temper and impatience flare up regularly, especially when the insects are irritating. There is a definite order of dominance among members of a group, with the stallion almost always at the top of the order. The mares, yearlings, and others occupy specific diminishing places of rank. Even though ponies assert their rank from time to time with threatening actions, there is little attempt to alter it except as young stallions challenge an older one for possession and domination of his mares. So the order of dominance for the most part is quite stable. As mares mature, they fit in at various levels depending upon the "personality" traits of each individual, traits that we cannot fathom but that are nonetheless real. Size differences may have something, but not everything, to do with this, while age apparently does not. If you watch ponies on the island for any length of time, you will surely see occasional threatening gestures. A dominant animal will stretch out its head with ears laid back and mouth open. If the challenge is a severe one, the pony is likely to strike out and attempt to bite its adversary.

Adult Assateague ponies are not prone to great activity. Their usual gait is simply a slow and purposeful walk from one grazing area to another, generally in single file in approximate order of dominance, with the stallion leading. At times a pony may trot to where others are already feeding, but only rarely do you see the entire group canter or gallop along the sands. When they do it is a memorable sight full of fluid motion and freedom, as they drift lightly over their barren, open homeland, sometimes showing high spirits by leaping and kicking out with their hind legs. Moving from one area to another is not

Mutual grooming (top) is by invitation and involves nibbling the mane and neck, either ritually or to remove insects. Sometimes horses will stand head-to-toe to keep flies off each other's heads by swishing their tails. When greenhead flies are bad at the height of summer, ponies may retreat to the beach (middle) and even enter the surf for relief. Rolling (bottom) is another way to combat insects.

These island "ponies" are actually small horses. Pony is a term used to designate horses smaller than 14 hands. True ponies have genetic distinctions beyond their size. The free-roaming animals of Assateague have been called ponies by generations of nearby Chincoteague residents and by children everywhere who have read Marguerite Henry's classic book Misty of Chincoteague.

always as haphazard as it appears on these wide-open spaces. Frequently the group or even the entire herd is urged toward a specific region by the stallion, who stays to the rear rather than leading his charges. You can identify this shepherding behavior when he is behind the others with his ears laid back, his head stretched out close to the ground and swaying back and forth. This form of equine behavior is known as "snaking."

One of the most enjoyable sights of pony-watching is young foals and colts at play. Like youngsters everywhere, the foals are exuberant: they jump and kick, buck into the air, or gallop in circles around a harassed but patient mother. Everything is new to the foals, and, nibbling and sniffing, they must investigate all sorts of objects on the interdune flats and along the beach. They play with one another, pretending to fight and rearing up to paw the air with their front legs. When a stallion passes by, they quiet down and show great interest; but they stay close to their mothers.

Campers on the island are sometimes startled late at night by strange and unexpected sounds close to their tents. With only a little attention, it is possible to learn a bit of pony language and thus to determine what is going on in their society. Specialists in animal behavior around the world, especially those working in England and Africa among the zebras, have identified specific equine sounds, all of which are clearly recognizable among Assateague ponies. Perhaps the most common call is the *nicker*, a rather deep, throaty sound. It is used under a wide variety of conditions: if a foal strays too far away from its mother, the mare may call out with a nicker, answered almost at once by a higher pitched nicker from the foal. It is a call used primarily to make contact. It is also a comment on a strange object seen for the first time, such as an approaching beach walker or a dog or some other animal, so it serves as a mild alarm signal as well. Because a nicker is used when people draw near, we obviously hear it more frequently than other pony sounds. Nickers are also used to answer the *whinny*, which essentially is only a higher, louder version of the nicker. This call carries much greater distances and may be used as a genuine call from one animal to another; often a mare to a foal lost to her sight over the dunes. Each

A lone pony in shaggy winter coat grazes against the frozen backdrop of Chincoteague Bay. Assateague ponies have reverted to basic types suited to severe conditions and resemble wild Asian horses more than modern domestic ones.

animal has an individual voice and, although they all sound alike to human ears, each animal recognizes members of its own group or family. A foal instantly identifies its mother's whinny.

There are other, less commonly heard sounds. Stallions make distinctive snorting noises when they are threatening to fight or when approaching a mare in heat. If a true fight develops between two stallions, they may utter a shrill squeal or scream, a sound that is heard for great distances. Should a fight develop near a campground at night, momentarily terrified campers will have a hard time getting back to sleep! Mares may squeal too when, if they are in heat, they are approached by a stallion or are engaged in a brief fight with one another.

But pony language is not all sound. There are body and facial expressions that carry meaning as well. When a male draws near a female in heat, she may paw the air with her foreleg, a distinctive motion uncommon at other times. Anyone who knows horses well understands most of the facial expressions seen in domestic as well as in wild animals. Yawning, for example, occurs as it does in us, before or after a period of rest, or in foals after suckling. To some degree this aids in encouraging circulation in facial muscles after relaxation. But mares may also yawn frequently when they are in heat, which could be an invitation for mating. A pony's yawn consists of cocking its ears forward, opening its mouth and exposing both upper and lower teeth, in contrast to the grooming invitation when only the lower teeth are exposed. Still another variation consists of opening the mouth and curling back the upper lip, revealing only the upper teeth. This expression seems to be related to testing a particular odor that has meaning, such as territorial marking by excretions, or mares in heat.

A greeting expression when two members of the same group approach one another calls for extending the head with ears cocked forward, a situation that may then develop into an invitation for mutual grooming. In a threat gesture, ears are laid back and the mouth is slightly opened. If the threat persists, a pony's ears go flat back, and almost immediately there may be a lunge and a bite.

The final expression, known as snapping, consists of ears laid part way back, neck stretched out straight, and a chewing motion with teeth covered but lips drawn back on the sides. This occurs before or after mutual grooming, or among young colts if they feel threatened by another pony. A colt approaching an older pony may snap in a kind of nervous anticipation before inviting mutual grooming.

Even though the origin of the Assateague ponies is rooted in a distant domesticated past, these animals are wild in every sense of the word and are the only large, unaffected animals along the East Coast that can be seen easily and safely at close range. Early in this century Virginians began introducing some domestic brood stock which, to a certain degree, has affected the physical traits of the ponies, especially those at the southern end. The northern ponies have been left largely alone ever since 1965. Nevertheless, many of the Assateague ponies, with their stocky physique and heavy coats, resemble the wild horses of Asia more closely than they resemble modern domestic ones. Their breeding went on for centuries uncontrolled by man, so their pool of genes or hereditary traits has allowed them to revert to a basic type well-suited to life under severe environmental conditions. Weak and unfit individuals, unable to survive the stresses, were weeded out long ago by natural processes. What we have left today is a remarkably sturdy creature that is as much a part of barrier-island life as anything that lived there long before man arrived on the continent.

The management of wild ponies for visitor safety and as a natural resource offers unique challenges for the U.S. Fish and Wildlife Service and the National Park Service. A free brochure detailing current practices is available at visitor centers.

Index

Numbers in italics refer to photographs, illustrations, or maps

Ocean City Inlet 31, 40, 44-45
Osprey 82, 112, 115
Owl, great horned 81-82
Oysters 19, 22, 39

Peat, marsh 45
Pine, loblolly *81*
Pine forest zone 81-84
Pirates 16, 19
Plants 41, 58, *68-69, 86, 87,* 88;
aquatic, 45; 71-72, 103-4; in
interdune zone, 63-64, 65,
66-67; in salt marsh. *See also*
Algae; Beachgrass; Cordgrass;
Poison ivy
Plover, piping *56*
Pocomoke River 1ι2
Poison ivy 72, 75, 81
Ponds 71-74, 109, 112, 115
Ponies 60, 80, 118-25; in
interdune zone, 64; in pine for-
est zone, 83; in saltmarsh, 91;
origins on Chincoteague, 14-15;
photos of, *8-9, 116-17, 122*
Pope Island 19, 44
Portuguese-man-o'-war 98

Recreation 23; beachwalking,
28-30
Redcedar 81
Reptiles 80, 81, 82

Salt 22, 29, 41, 61-62
Saltmarsh 41, 83, 119; animals
in, 91-92, 93; formation and
character of, 45, 84, 85-86, 87;
plantlife on, *86, 87,* 88, 90-91,
93, 99
Saltmeadow hay *See* Cordgrass
Sand 61, 62, 70; deposits and
movement of, 37, 39-40, 45, 52,
58-59, 81; formation of, 31, 46
Sandpiper *56,* 58
Sandy Point 44
Scallop 99, *102*
Scarp 51
Seaboard Oil and Guano Com-
pany 19, 22

Seal, harbor *42-43*
Seashore, national 114
Shipwrecks 14
Shorebirds 53, 58, 112
Shrimp 99, *102,* 105
Shrubs 83. *See also* Thicket
zone
Sinepuxent Bay 94
Skimmer *39,* 61
Slough Inlet 44
Snakes *See* Reptiles
Spiders 63
Squirrel, Delmarva Peninsula
fox, *81,* 115
Starling 119
Storms 39, 40, 59, 83; damage
caused by, 13-14, 22, *30;* effect
on barrier island, 44, 45, 50, 51,
72. *See also* Hurricanes
Sugar Point Cove 44
Swan, tundra *113*

Teach, Edward (Blackbeard) 16
Temperature 47, 62, 70. *See
also* Weather
Tern, *57,* 58, 61
Terrapin, diamondback 19
Thicket zone 71, 74-75, 80-81
Tides 41, 44, 45, 99, 103
Toad, Fowler's 80, 82
Toms Cove 19, 22, 39, *42,* 44
Trees *See* Pine forest zone
Topography 22

Undertow 50-51

Voyage to Virginia, A 12

Warbler, Swainson's 115
Wash Flats 44
Washington Canyon 31
Wasp 65, 70
Waterfowl 19, 104; in Chin-
coteague National Wildlife Ref-
uge, 112
Waves *31-32,* 39, 50-52, 59
Weather 22-23. *See also* Hurri-
canes; Storms

Wicomico 13
Widgeongrass 103-4
Wildlife refuges 114, 115. *See
also* Chincoteague National
Wildlife Refuge
Winds 47, 62
Winter Quarter Gut 44
Worm, peacock 99, *102*

Handbook 106

The National Park Service expresses its appreciation to all those persons who made the preparation and production of this handbook possible.

All photography or other artwork not credited below comes from the files of Assateague Island National Seashore and the National Park Service.

William H. Amos 66-67; 68 ferns; 69 lichen, beach rose, saltwort; 81; 86; 87; 96; 97; 100-102; 113 bottom; and 122 top, bottom.

R. Hill 30.

Helen Schreider 69 thistle.